# I NEVER KNOWED IT WAS HARD

# I NEVER KNOWED IT WAS HARD

## *Memoirs of a Labrador Trapper*

Louie Montague

*Edited by* Elizabeth Dawson

*Foreword by* Keith Chaulk

*Introduction by* Robin McGrath

ISER

Institute of Social and Economic Research

Fifth printing, 2021



Louie Montague, Elizabeth Dawson, and ISER Books gratefully acknowledge the financial support of a Health Canada grant awarded to Sivunivut Inuit Community Corporation of North West River and assistance by the Labrador Institute of Memorial University.

**Library and Archives Canada Cataloguing in Publication**

Montague, Louie, 1935-

I never knowed it was hard : memoirs of a Labrador trapper / Louie Montague ; edited by Elizabeth Dawson.

Includes bibliographical references.

ISBN 978-1-894725-12-5

1. Montague, Louie, 1935-. 2. Trappers--Newfoundland and Labrador--Labrador--Biography. 3. Inuit--Newfoundland and Labrador--Labrador--Biography. 4. Labrador (N.L.)--Biography. I. Dawson, Elizabeth, 1950- II. Title.

SK283.6.C2M65 2013 639'.1092 C2013-900585-4

(Social and economic studies; 74)

Cover photo: Louie Montague filing an axe in front of his tilt, Naskaupi River, September 2012. Photo: E. Dawson.
Back cover photo: Model of toboggan and typical trapper's load, by Louie Montague. Photo: E. Dawson.
Snowshoes image: McCord Museum M986.67.6.A-B
Design: Alison Carr
Copy editing: Richard Tallman

Published by ISER Books, an imprint of Memorial University Press
Institute of Social and Economic Research
Memorial University of Newfoundland
St. John's, NL A1C 5S7
www.memorialuniversitypress.ca
Printed and bound in Canada

# CONTENTS

*Foreword* / Keith Chaulk .......... 7
*Editor's Preface* .......... 9
*Acknowledgements* .......... 14
*Introduction* / Robin McGrath .......... 15

1 Early Memories .......... 21
2 Family History .......... 36
3 Early Trapping Years .......... 43
4 More Trapping .......... 54
5 Naskaupi River .......... 66
6 Working on the Base .......... 82
7 Other Jobs .......... 90
8 Salmon Fishing .......... 104
9 Seal Hunting and Dogs .......... 107
10 Caribou Hunting in the Mealies .......... 122
11 Traplines and Custom Law .......... 138
12 Innu .......... 145
13 Music, Fiddle Playing, and Memories of Fiddlers .......... 152
14 Later Years .......... 160

Appendix 1: Typical Day on the Trapline .......... 167
Appendix 2: Supplies for the Trapline .......... 169
Appendix 3: Trapper's Tilt .......... 170

*Glossary* .......... 171
*References* .......... 179

# FOREWORD

*Keith Chaulk*

I first read Louie Montague's book, *I Never Knowed It Was Hard*, after I was contacted in 2011 for advice on publishing and was sent a brief excerpt for review. After reading only a few lines, I heard the voice of my father, my grandfathers, and my friends. North West River people have a certain way of speaking, and it really comes across in Louie's storytelling. It was the first time I had read a book chapter and experienced that feeling; needless to say, I was hooked right away.

For me, reading Louie's story was very much like listening to him talk, to the point that my ears perked up when I read that Louie's grandfather named traps after the kids. My father did the same thing. It never occurred to me that this might be a local tradition. This is one of the many valuable contributions Louie's story makes; he informs some of us about our own culture, while for others he provides insights that might otherwise soon be lost.

During their prime, Louie worked together with my father fighting fires throughout Labrador. In those days, Wildlife and Forestry were the same department. After the summer fire season was over, they would spend the rest of the year on wildlife patrol and/or helping biologists conduct their field research.

Louie tells one story about a time when Silas Baikie and my father were out on boat patrol. Their outboard motors failed, and they swamped from behind. Silas decided to stay with the boat, while my father chose to swim for shore. Five days later it was Louie and an RCMP search plane that found my father. Silas did not make it. It was in the fall of 1969, the year I was born.

Twenty plus years later, Louie became my boss. In 1991, Percy Montague, Kathleen ("Cat") Cooper, Louie, and I were hired to clean up an old

American recreation camp located near the Rapids on the north side of Grand Lake. They were proposing to establish a provincial park. Louie, who had just retired from Forestry, was the foreman and oldest, while I was back from studying at Dalhousie University for the summer and was the youngest.

We'd go to work every morning in a speedboat and work outdoors all day. If it rained hard we would burn brush and take turns sitting around in the tent talking, playing cards, smoking, and drinking tea. Louie told a lot of stories that summer, about the old days and people we knew. It was one of the best jobs I ever had. It was a good summer. I could not have asked for a better group to work with. Percy and Cat have both since passed, but fortunately Louie is still with us. This book is a testament to his life; however, it would not have seen the light of day without the hard work of Elizabeth Dawson, who recorded Louie's stories, transcribed his words, and pushed to have it published.

I believe that this book is a valuable record of recent Labrador history as seen through the eyes of one man. For me, it has been a pleasure and privilege to read and I can only hope that others will enjoy it half as much.

Dr. Keith Chaulk is Director of the Labrador Institute of Memorial University.

# EDITOR'S PREFACE

Louie Montague was born in North West River on Valentine's Day, 1935. He lived the traditional life of a Labrador trapper while supplementing his income with seasonal work at the newly established air base in Goose Bay and by working as a prospector, guide, and geologist's helper as the resources of Labrador were explored and mapped. He sought further education and had a 30-year career with the provincial government in the natural resources sectors. Louie's knowledge of the land was a significant asset to his understanding of the management of Labrador resources and was recognized by his employers as bringing a unique approach to management. Seldom before had Labrador people been employed in management capacities or offered the chance to advance, especially as educational opportunities at that time were only available far from the life they loved and the land they travelled. During his work career, Louie continued to hunt and trap in his spare time, both to supplement his income and diet, and to pursue his passion to be on the land.

I was a nurse from Ontario who came to North West River in 1976 to work with the Grenfell Mission and married Louie's friend and next-door neighbour, Brian Michelin. Louie's wife Ruth became my mentor in all things concerning keeping a Labrador home. Our families visited back and forth over the years and I listened to Brian and Louie and others share stories around the kitchen table about their lives and about the land.

I developed a great respect for Louie's honesty and integrity and his gifts as a storyteller. While Louie's lifestyle was similar to that of his peers, his stories always had a quality and clarity about them that set them apart. Beyond merely describing what he had seen and experienced during his travels in the country, he explained the science behind many of these phenomena and brought a unique understanding to telling them. As a natural teacher, he demonstrated patience in explaining and answering questions, sometimes coming back later with the comment, "I've been thinking about what we were talking about and looked it up [in such and such a book, or he called someone to ask about it] and this is what I found out." His stories were honest and without embellishment, and he often laughed at himself and some of the situations he got into — and out of. His memory was formidable.

Appreciating the gifts of other storytellers, Louie has long been an avid collector and reader of books and articles about Labrador, in addition to devotedly reading the quarterly periodical *Them Days*. He devours this material and fills in gaps in his knowledge of his family and Labrador history, gains new understanding of the context of events, and furthers his understanding of traditional practices. Hence, as a "traditional" narrator of his own and others' experiences, and of his love of the land, Louie is very much an educated and "modern" storyteller whose sources extend beyond the oral tradition of told and retold stories, just as traditional folksingers often have in their repertoires songs, such as country and western songs and murder ballads, that they learned from radio or from print sources.[1]

His well-worn copies of *Them Days* bear his personal notes, cross-references, underlining, and comments. Stories from people living in other northern regions also aid his understanding and are of great interest to him. A special delight was finding the book *Some Things I Have Done*, by Randle F. Holme, which included a chapter on Holme's travels on the Grand River (now Churchill) with John Montague, Louie's great-grandfather and the first Montague to come to Labrador, as well as some previously unseen photos of John Montague. Discovering *Northern Quebec and Labrador Journals and Correspondence 1819-35*, published for the Hudson's Bay Company in London in 1963, has also been a great resource for Louie's better understanding of life in the North. Over the years academics, adventurers, and journalists have contacted Louie to ask him to explain some recent natural event or change in trends, to verify stories told by others, or to seek advice about travel into the country around the Naskaupi River.

After talking to Louie, they invariably have told him that he should write a book. Several offered to help but got the standard reply, "What I did was no different than anybody else them days."

With retirement ahead of me in January 2011, I asked my son, Ossie Michelin, for a digital recorder for Christmas. I had prepared Louie, who by this time was my beloved partner and companion, following the deaths of our spouses (Ruth in 2001 and Brian in 2003), telling him that recording his memoirs was on my retirement "to do" list. In preparing for this undertaking, I didn't research tape recording or transcribing, but I have always been a "word nerd" and enjoyed writing, and reading all the Labrador books, and so I believed this was something that we could do together. I told him that all he had to do was talk and that I would transcribe and edit. Understanding that his stories could be of value to the next generations and to people who don't know Labrador as he does, he agreed to try. As Louie talked and committed himself to remembering and explaining details, I believe he gained confidence that his familiarity with the land made him well suited for this task. As I recorded the story, I became even more convinced that, indeed, his story had to be told, especially the story of life on the Naskaupi River. Many people lived through the same changing times but few have articulated the impact these changes have had.

Throughout the early months of 2011, I would go to Louie's house or he would come to my house, we would get comfortable, and then I would say "Tell me a story" and he would begin and continue with very little prompting. He even began to make notes during the daytime of topics he wanted to be sure to cover that night. He often called his friends and cousins, especially Bernard Chaulk and Wilbert Montague, to check facts. They would remind him of details he had forgotten and set him off on further remembrances.

As Louie recorded the stories in the evenings, I transcribed them the next day, and this process continued for about four months. Then began the editing process. I wanted to keep Louie's voice intact, so changed his words very little indeed, except for removing the occasional false starts. I merely organized the material into chapters with common themes. There were times when he really got rolling and then self-edited, saying, "You can't put that in; it might offend someone." So, unfortunately, some of the juicier tales are not included in this book. After the manuscript had been organized into chapters, Louie read the hard copy and pencilled in comments, made notes to himself to explain further, and deleted parts; together we identified words that needed to be included in a Glossary. He identified what needed to be included in the appendices and handwrote the material for the appendices, saying he was glad he didn't have to handwrite the entire book. In a number of places, I pushed him to explain certain aspects, arguing that "no, everybody doesn't know what that means."

There are many more stories. More recently, since I completed the process of transcribing and editing and had a first draft of the manuscript, Louie has continued to tell me new stories and I will scribble notes on hotel stationery, restaurant napkins, fly leaves of books, or odd bits of paper until I can get home and add them to the manuscript. We haven't done any further recording, but have expanded these notes into some additional stories. As recently as September 2012, on a goose hunting trip to the Naskaupi River, Louie remembered and sang part of a forgotten verse for "Me and Aukie and Grampa" as we steamed slowly down Hegrew Lake. Sometimes he'll say, "That's not a story. Nobody cares about that stuff." That is when I remind him of details that would be important to know about his own history, however trivial. Of particular interest to me is when he mentions the names of people, and places them in the context of his life and time. I understand that these details may be important to others who are also trying to fill in the blanks in their own history.

In this regard, the Glossary at the end of book aims to provide some background on those individuals who, directly or indirectly, are part of Louie's story and who also have become part of the larger historical narrative of Labrador. In addition, the Glossary explains the many local terms that are part of Louie's narrative, as well as place names that otherwise might not be recognized. All of these Glossary terms and names, where they first appear in the text, are in boldface so readers can readily check meanings and/or further historical detail.

Louie's one regret when working on this project was that he hadn't asked more questions, particularly during the lifetimes of his parents, grandparents, and his Uncle Austin Montague. He acknowledges that in his younger days he either didn't take the time to ask or, perhaps, to listen to stories being told. He often says that if only they had written it all down, how much richer his understanding would be now. Thankfully, *Them Days* has preserved stories from these and other individuals and it is there that Louie turns for information and clarification.

Louie still says that he didn't do anything different from others of his generation. I think he did. After learning and living the traditional ways, Louie left them behind for two years to study forest and wildlife management in St. John's. Equally important as his desire to learn more and get ahead in his career were the support and encouragement of his late wife, Ruth Andersen Montague, who kept the home fires burning, literally, and that was no small task in those times. Undoubtedly, the educational background that he achieved during his studies and later on the job, coupled with his thirst to understand what he was seeing in the natural world, has given him a unique understanding and the ability to both examine and explain what others may have taken for granted.

Louie has lived through some remarkable changes in the social and physical and political world of Labrador, and his story captures these as he describes their impact on his life and the lives of those around him — people, as well as the land and the animals. His vibrant connection to the land, especially the Naskaupi River, continues to this day, and it is there that he returns whenever he can.

— Elizabeth Dawson

---

Note

1. I am grateful to the ISER Books editor, Dr. Richard Tallman, for this insight.

# ACKNOWLEDGEMENTS

This book has been 77 years in the making. I didn't know anything about writing a book and really appreciate the people who helped. Keith Chaulk and Martha MacDonald at the Labrador Institute gave me encouragement. The staff at the Institute of Social and Economic Research (ISER) at Memorial University were very professional and helpful. Robin McGrath read an early draft and was the person to make that important first connection with ISER. Robin continued to read our work, make suggestions, and gave great encouragement.

Bernard Chaulk and Wilbert Montague were always ready to talk over old times and I depended on their memories for a lot of these stories. Their memories are better than mine and they're born storytellers. We had some good laughs. I wish they'd write their own books. So many of the old trappers are gone but I think about them every day and all the stories I heard from them and the things I learned from them. I'm so thankful *Them Days* has kept their stories alive.

I appreciate my family: my brothers and sisters and my children and grandchildren and the time I had with Ruth. It's because of family that we did what we did them days; it's because of family that I write these memoirs so that they will have this story in their hands. I wish some of my ancestors had written it all down for me.

And then, there's Liz. Without her, this book never would have happened. I never would have spent the time or had the patience to do all this work. She kept the ball rolling and explained the details to me. She made me work hard and think even harder. I thank her with all my heart.

— Louie Montague

# INTRODUCTION

*Robin McGrath*

The Quebec-Labrador Peninsula, in the northeast of North America between Hudson Bay and the Gulf of St. Lawrence, is the country Jacques Cartier famously called "The Land God Gave to Cain." The Atlantic side of this peninsula, today part of the Canadian province of Newfoundland and Labrador, consists of approximately 300,000 square kilometres of mountains, rivers, coastal islands, forests, and barren lands. This is the infertile land God is said to have condemned Cain to till as punishment for the murder of his brother. This is Louie Montague's home.

The earliest people began living in Labrador shortly after the glaciers retreated, and left traces of their culture in the Strait of Belle Isle area approximately 9,000 years ago. The Labrador Archaic (Indian) tradition has been identified by archaeologists as present about 1,500 years later in the L'Anse Amour area on the Strait of Belle Isle coast in southern Labrador, and by 4,000 years ago the culture of the Pre-Dorset had developed to become what is known as the Dorset, and some time later the Subarctic people, the Innu, appeared. By the time the Vikings made their way to the Wunderstrands on Labrador's southeast coast around AD 1000, the Thule, the ancestors of the modern-day Inuit, were moving steadily eastward across the Arctic, and eventually displaced the Dorset along the Labrador coast. While the Innu (formerly called the Montagnais and Naskapi) hunted the interior and the Thule relied to a greater extent on sea mammals, in certain respects they shared parts of the same territory. By the year AD 1500, Europeans were beginning to make their way in greater numbers into Labrador to add to the mix, and the Thule culture was evolving to what we today call the Inuit.

The Innu, the Inuit, the French, and the Scots: these were the cultural and genetic ancestors of trapper Louie Montague, author of these memoirs.

By the time Louie was born at North West River in 1935, the Labrador trappers had developed a multi-ethnic society that incorporated traditions from all these societies. Marriage to Aboriginal women enabled European trappers to gain the knowledge, skills, and support necessary to survival for them and their descendants. They used the sweat lodges and hunting terminology of the Innu; they adopted Inuit sleds and clothing; and they employed European guns and steel traps.

For over four centuries these people, who called themselves Settlers, pursued their livelihoods with innovation and adaptation, adopting whatever cultural practices and artifacts made living in the Labrador interior possible.

However, as fur prices dropped and other means of earning a living became available, trapping as a lifestyle began to die off. The songs, stories, clothing, rituals, and knowledge that made the trappers unique began to disappear with the old-timers, but they left a lasting cultural legacy in Newfoundland and Labrador, a legacy that is still alive for Louie Montague and a handful of other men and women who lived the trapping life in their youth.

By taking up trapping Louie Montague was following an ancient tradition. Fur-bearing animals were caught by Aboriginal people in Labrador from the earliest time. Prior to the introduction of metal traps, Innu and Inuit used stones and trees to create deadfall traps, traded for or made spears and arrowheads for killing caribou and seals, and used the meat for food and the skins and furs for clothing, tools, and shelter.

Trapping solely for fur as a trade item came to Labrador with the Europeans. Seasonal workers, such as the Basques and the West Country English, trapped on the Labrador coast from the 1500s, and in time trading began to draw Aboriginal people from the interior. Inuit began trapping foxes for trade in the Lake Melville area around the year 1600, and Louis Fornel, a French trader, founded the first year-round trading post in Hamilton Inlet in 1743 at North West River. In 1836, the Hudson's Bay Company purchased the post and dominated the fur trade in that area until 1901, when Revillon Frères broke the HBC monopoly, resulting in better fur prices for the trappers.

Better prices did not always coincide with better catches, however, and trapping provided a very precarious living for Settler families. Due to the cyclical nature of the fur-bearing animal populations and the fickle fashion industry of Europe, starvation threatened all those Labradorians who trapped and hunted for a living. Low fur markets after World War I and in the late 1930s and early 1940s had a negative effect on trappers' incomes.

World War II changed that situation dramatically. In 1941, the American military began constructing a major air base at Goose Bay, 45 kilometres east of Louie's home at North West River, and year-round work for wages became available. Within a short time, many Labradorians had made the adjustment from mixed, seasonal employment to full-time work throughout the year. Trapping became a "hobble," a part-time job mostly done by retired men and seasonal or shift workers. Louie was one of those who struggled to keep the trapping life going, but his natural work ethic and ambition led him reluctantly away from the land. It was some years before he restored balance to his life by using his knowledge and skills gained as a trapper in his work as a trained forest technician.

Travel on the river was exhausting and fraught with danger. Some men faced illness or starvation alone in their tilts; some men drowned in the rapids, or at best lost their season's catch to fire or accident. Yet despite the brutal work and the harsh conditions, many men, and a few women, were emotionally and spiritually attached to the life and the land. Some trappers dreaded the commencement of the trapping season, but others longed for it and the tremendous sense of freedom and peace they experienced when they were on their traplines in the bush.

Many people have written about the Labrador trapping life over the last several centuries. Some, like Captain George Cartwright (*A Journal of Transaction . . . on the Coast of Labrador*, 1792) and Elliott Merrick (*True North*, 1933), were sojourners who spent some time in the country but ultimately left. Others, including Horace Goudie (*Trails to Remember*, 1991), Harold Paddon (*Green Woods and Blue Waters*, 1989), and Chesley Lethbridge (*A Life of Challenge*, 2007), told the story from the point of view of native-born sons. Paulus Maggo (*Remembering the Years of My*

*Life*, 1999, an oral history translated from Inuktitut), John Poker (Henriksen, *I Dreamed the Animals*, 2008, recorded in Innu-aimun), and Matthew Mestokosho (Bouchard, *Caribou Hunter*, 2004, recorded in Innu-aimun, translated first into French, and then into English) give the Aboriginal perspective.

Some of what we know today about the trappers comes from the affidavits collected as part of the legal case related to the Labrador Boundary Dispute. After geologist A.P. Low described the huge potential of water power, timber, and iron ore deposits he observed in the Labrador interior in the mid-1890s, Ottawa attempted to usurp these resources by arbitrarily moving the Quebec-Labrador boundary northward. It was testimony from trappers such as John Michelin and John Blake, who wished Labrador to be considered part of Canada ("In the Matter of the Boundary"), as well as those such as Henry Webb and John Winter, who felt that Canada had no claim to the area at all ("Privy Council Affidavits"), that secured the interior of Labrador for Newfoundland.

Women, too, have had their say about the trapping life. Lydia Campbell (*Sketches of Labrador Life*, 1894-95), Margaret Baikie (*Labrador Memories*, n.d.), and Elizabeth Goudie (*Woman of Labrador*, 1973) were all trappers in their own right, but they were also the wives of trappers and knew what it was to be on the waiting end of the traplines. Visitors such as Mina Hubbard (*A Woman's Way through Unknown Labrador*, 1908) and Kate Austen (Merrick, *Northern Nurse*, 1942) gave the outsiders' perspective.

A few traders — the middle-men who bought the furs — have left accounts of their work also. William O.K. Ross's travel journal describes the 1,600-kilometre buying trip he made on foot from Quebec City in 1909 (Smith, 2003). Leonard Budgell, born in Labrador, ran Hudson's Bay Company trading posts all across Canada's North (Budgell, 2009).

What makes Louie Montague's account unique is the way he goes into specific detail about the material culture, the language, the clothing, the education process, and the daily life of a trapper. Unlike many hunters who know what they are talking about, this author also realizes that his reader may not be familiar with the basic elements of what he is describing, so he explains not just what he did but also why and how he did it.

Another element that makes this memoir stand out is Louie's willingness to explore his status as a Labrador Settler—part Inuit, part European, with perhaps a little Innu and Cree mixed in. Other Settlers who have written about their lives have tended to suppress or exaggerate their genetic inheritance. Ernie Lyall, author of *An Arctic Man* (1979), moved north from Labrador when he went to work for the Hudson's Bay Company, married an Inuk woman from Cape Dorset, and founded a family prominent in the political and business life of Nunavut. His Labrador relatives still don't understand why he claimed his Inuk mother, who taught him Inuktitut, was English. Sarah Elizabeth Ford, who wrote *Land of the Good Shadows* (Washburne and Anauta, 1940) and other books under the Inuit name Anauta, claimed to be fully Inuit, though she had, in fact, only an Inuk great-grandmother and was seven-eighths European.

Where other authors have fictionalized some of their experiences, Louie Montague's story is as authentic as frail human memory can make it. Where possible, he has confirmed his experiences from other documents, such as memoirs published in *Them Days* magazine. When he is unsure about a fact, he gives fair warning to his reader. He is concerned to be accurate and complete. He is recording what he believes to be the truth, rather then bending the truth to make a more rollicking story. This is what makes his work so valuable to scholars and academics, and so compelling to the general reader.

Dr. Robin McGrath is the author of the seminal study, *Canadian Inuit Literature: The Development of a Tradition* (1984), and has published numerous articles on Aboriginal issues. She lives in Goose Bay, Labrador.

Figure 1: Labrador. Map courtesy of Charles Conway.

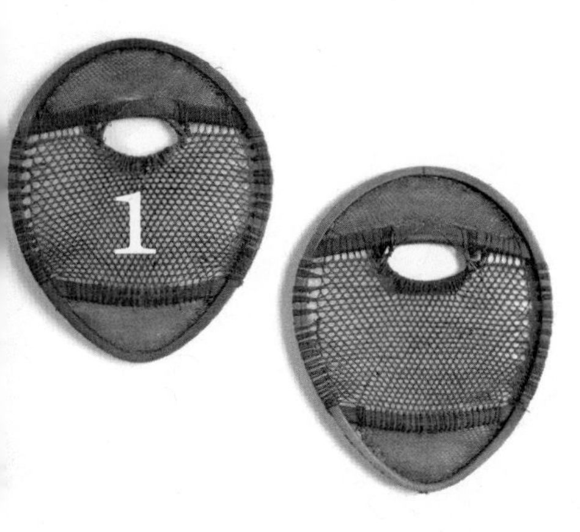

# 1 EARLY MEMORIES

Our family's main **tilt** was at the mouth of the Red Wine River where it enters the Naskaupi River. There's been a tilt there a long time; I can trace it back to 1858 or earlier. We lived up the Naskaupi River in this tilt a couple years from October to April, during the trapping season. I guess Father wanted us with him and since none of us was in school yet, we went with him. We went up by boat in October and Uncle Ike Rich and Uncle Harvey Montague came up with dog teams and brought us home in the spring.

I was probably three or four when I first remember being up there. There was our parents and Irene, Russell, and me. I remember a baby in a swing [baby's hammock] in the corner of the tilt. That would have been Pauline as she's next younger than me. I remember Uncle Arch Goudie was the next closest trapper, up at Hegrew Lake, an hour or so walk away. His place was where Lee Baikie and Val Ritch have their cabin now. He had his family up there, Aunt Lily and Milton, their adopted son. Milton was older than us and I remember me and my older brother Russell following him along the shore. Milton was old enough to shoot a gun and I remember him shooting muskrats. He'd shoot the muskrats and we'd try to get them with a long stick. Myself and Russell weren't old enough to use a gun yet. We never did any work on Sunday but we would go up to Uncle Arch and Aunt Lily's one Sunday, and the next Sunday they'd come down with us for the day. Aunt Lily was an awful good cook and she always made cookies for us; I can taste them and smell them yet. Aunt Lily and Uncle Arch were wonderful people.

Rabbits were really plentiful that fall; my father used to bring birch and spruce tree tops and put them right under the window of the cabin and on moonlight nights we would watch rabbits feeding on the tops, right under the window. That was really exciting! We used to slide in the snow on the bank and play on the ice. One time, somebody came out on the portage path and told us there was a live lynx in a trap on the hill. My father told my mother to take us children and go in and get the lynx. So we went in there with Mother and she shot the lynx in the trap with a .22 and brought it out. My father would leave us for five or six days and go on the cross-country trapline while we stayed at the cabin.

Father would take the whole family up Grand Lake or the Naskaupi River before trapping season opened in the fall. One time we went in a 14-foot rowboat. Henry Blake loaned us a 5-horsepower outboard motor and we went up the Red Wine River, berry-picking, and stayed in our tilt. There was an old **burn** up Red [Wine] River that was good for **redberries**; we climbed that big hill on the south side every morning to pick berries. That's where father had his bear traps because the bears were in there feeding on the berries. Mother and us children would be berry-picking and father would check his bear traps. There were lots of squash berries in Hegrew Lake and we picked them, too. He would also be hunting geese and ducks, and checking for signs of fur-bearing animals.

Sometimes we would come out to Black Point on Grand Lake, another redberry place; it's all growed up now. One time, we were camped in over the bank so we were a long way away from the boat; it was beautiful in there on the berry banks. We had barrels of berries for our winter food. In the night, a bad windstorm came on and the boat came ashore, and the barrels overturned; there were berries all over the place. The next day, we were picking up the berries out of the water and on the shore.

I went to Yale School in North West River for seven years; I think I was in Grade 8 when I quit and took off to the trapline. That was normal for us boys to go with our fathers on the traplines in them days. Some of the boys stayed on to Grade 11 and went away to get a higher education. When I was going to leave school, Mr. Hoyles called me into his office. He didn't want me to leave. He told me that I was doing the wrong thing; that trapping wouldn't always last. He tried to talk me into staying in school but I wouldn't listen. I saw the trappers coming home with big loads of fur and telling their yarns, and that's what I wanted.

Mr. Hoyles was the principal; we all liked him. He liked to hunt; he got a canoe for goose and duck hunting, and a dog team the first year he was here. One of his dogs was a reddish colour, very unusual looking. The school windows looked out on the river and one spring while Mr. Hoyles was teaching us, he saw a big company of ducks land over on the Innu side. He said that he would excuse anybody who wanted to go after them but we knew it was a company of wild **piebirds** and there was no use to go after them; we were all laughing about it. Lots of times, he'd be teaching and looking out the window and tell us he saw ducks or geese flying past. Mr. Hoyles had a family here and they built the house that Uncle Piercy Chaulk lived in later. It was five-by-five squared logs with **oakum** between the logs. He visited around among the people; he'd come to our house and talk to my father about trapping.

They must have been pretty good teachers them days as we all did pretty good out of it. When we were growing up, we didn't know much about the outside world except for Newfoundland cause that's where our teachers came from and that's all they taught us — about Corner Brook and woods operations, and the ***Kyle***. They knew very little about Labrador. We didn't have any maps; we didn't know where we were in the world, didn't know about the rest of the world. We heard about Nova Scotia, like when my father ordered things from there, but we had no idea where it was.

They taught us how to embroider at school. They would trace designs on the flaps of the pockets for the Grenfell parkas. We'd work at them at school and then take them home at night to finish. They gave us the silks [embroidery floss], the needles, everything to do it with. We'd take them [finished products] back to Mrs. Keddy at the handicraft store and she would give us some clothes in return, no money. Bill Michelin was a real good sewer; I remember him working at that. All of us would be at it when we were eight or nine years old. I remember one fall taking a half-gallon of redberries down to the Grenfell clothing store and getting a real nice cap, a high one like the police wear. I was some proud of it. Sometimes they would give us mitts or socks but Mother made most of those things for us.

My friends were Clayton Montague, Bill Michelin, and Aukie [Austin, Jr.] and Wilbert Montague. We used to play outdoors all the time, sliding on **komatiks**, making snowmen, diving in the snow. One time in the spring, I must have been seven or eight, the **Grenfell Mission** was fixing and painting their fences; me and some other kids were racing to school and a couple of the boys jumped over the fence and at the same time, I crawled through. The fence was apart and just standing there and when I crawled through, part of the fence with nails sticking out came down on my head and gave me a bad cut. Hugh Campbell was there working for the Mission and he seen what happened and picked me up in his arms and carried me to the hospital to get fixed up. I might have been knocked out for a few seconds. I still have the scar and barbers always ask me what happened. Another time I was cutting tree roots with a pocket knife and the knife slipped and went into my knee. Aunt Mary Montague [wife of Uncle Harvey] took me to the hospital to get fixed up. When we got to the hospital, I remember a nurse looked after me and she scrunched up Aspirin tablets and put them in the cut and dressed it and sent me on my way. I still got that scar, too.

I remember cleaning out the molasses barrels, puncheons, huge things, big enough for us little fellas to crawl into, and eating "sugar molasses" after the **HBC** [Hudson's Bay Company] was finished with them. When it was cold in the winter, they couldn't get all the molasses out of the puncheons. We'd go at them with spoons, took a spoon down with us purpose for doing that.

In my class at school were Mina [Blake] Hibbs, Rhyna McLean, Clayton Montague, Tommy Blake, Oscar Michelin, Florence Goudie, Jim Michelin,

Herb Blake, Florence Blake, Leslie Best, and a lot from **the Coast** who stayed in **the Dorm**. I remember Bert Sheppard and Sid Blake from Rigolet and young Joe Michelin from Traverspine. Tommy Blake died of diphtheria when we were real young and they had us walk by his grave and drop white flowers into it.

When I was school-aged, I went around with Grandfather Montague, camping up around Grand Lake and down around **the Islands**. We'd go trapping in the fall on Grand Lake, then setting trout nets down to Butter and Snow in the spring. Sometimes he'd take me and Aukie, Clayton, and Wilbert. We'd put up a tent for the night. He had a house at **the Rapids** where we'd stay overnight; he stayed up there in the summer, caught salmon and salted it for the Hudson's Bay Company, but the fisheries warden cut it out before my time [described in **Raoul Thevenet**'s statement to the **Privy Council** re the Labrador boundary dispute in 1921]. My grandfather learned me a lot; he was good at explaining things.

We had a motorboat and myself and Russell used it; sometimes we took Grandfather with us. Our parents found that good for Grandfather to go with us. The first one we had was a 29-foot open motorboat with a 6.5 Acadia motor; nobody could keep up with us. Later we got a 44-footer and Russell and me used it a lot; sometimes we went outside Rigolet hunting in the fall; then we'd go to Kenamu for commercial salmon fishing, go wherever we wanted to. My father used it to take surveyors and prospectors around but I never went on those trips.

Grandfather Montague had a fair-sized motorboat, kind of a schooner-type thing. In the fall he used to go outside Rigolet after fish [cod] and he used to do some fishing for the merchants in Indian Harbour. One was a fella named Jerrett. I've read in some books about him; he was a merchant from Newfoundland. I often heard Grandfather talk about Mr. Jerrett. Mr. Jerrett's son calls me once in a while and we have a great chat. He's over 80 years old, lives in Newfoundland. He has a diary his father kept when he was living here and trapping up at Sand Banks with the Michelins. Mr. Jerrett was married to Uncle Stewart's sister, Ruth.

I remember Grandfather's old motorboat, hauled up on the bank by our house where it rotted away. It had a cabin on it and us kids used to play there. I remember Grandmother and Grandfather living in their house near us; us kids would go down there every night. Grandfather used to love playing cards, "120s" and "45." They had a two-storey house; Grandfather and Uncle Austin built it. Then they built another house for Uncle Austin when he was first married; the houses were built of logs.

Grandfather was a very lucky trapper; he trapped Horseshoe Rapid on **Grand River**. Uncle Austin trapped with him there for 20 years, and then Uncle Harvey took over. Uncle Austin left there and went to Nipishish. I'm not sure that old John Montague, my great-grandfather, ever trapped; he was busy working for the HBC; and then he died so young, drowned in Gull Island Rapid.

After Grandfather got too old to trap Horseshoe Rapid, he trapped at the Rapids at the lower end of Grand Lake; that was his homestead, on the south side of the Rapids. He trapped all around there. He and Grandmother stayed there most of the trapping season and he'd tend traps five or six miles up Grand Lake on either side. He'd be gone for a night, staying in tent. I often stayed with them. We'd go up on weekends. He was a wonderful man to teach us kids.

I'll never forget him teaching us how to sail. He used to always sail when the wind was the right way, with one mast, one sail, and a line on it for hauling it around. We sailed in Grand Lake, around the trapline when we could; it was just a rowboat with a sail on it, and a set of oars. Everybody used a sail whenever they could. I always think about us sailing down Grand Lake with Grandfather one time, me and Aukie, and it was coming on a blow. We were going pretty wild and the boat would go over on its side with the sail almost touching the water, and he'd tell me and Aukie, "the jib, the jib," but we didn't know what that was, so we were grabbing at everything. He'd call out "the jib boom," but we didn't know what that was, either.

Me and Aukie and Clayton and Wilbert always went around with Grandfather, whoever could climb aboard. Grandmother stayed at the cabin but she never went around in the boat with him, not in my time. I don't remember him ever going up to the head of Grand Lake.

Grandfather taught us all about camping in tents, us little boys, how to get wood and what kind of wood to get and how to set traps. He had a trap named for all of us up Grand Lake, "Louie's trap," "Aukie's trap," "Clayton's trap," and so on. My trap was on the south side on the first cliff. I was some excited to go check my trap! We all had traps set around town here when we were little boys going to school, just six or seven years old. Some years when the foxes were plenty, I did real good right on the hill behind where my house is now. Mother had traps set all around, too. There was a foot trail that followed the hill in; it was called the "wood path" and it started where Russell's house is now. We went in there and set rabbit snares and checked them every morning before we went to school.

We were young when we went in canoes: seven or eight; we had guns, too. I find it strange now that people can't use guns until they're 16 or older. They didn't tell us "you're old enough now"; we just got in the canoe and went. There were a few motorboats around but it was mostly canoes; hunting was the only thing we ever heard of — that's what we were interested in. We listened to all the trappers' stories and grew up with our heads filled with that.

Me and Aukie or Clayton would go in canoe and set rabbit snares; we'd go right around the lake looking for ducks or **nansearies**, or **partridge** in the fall. We'd go across on the head over there [across Little Lake], a good place for spruce partridge; we'd go up in the brooks for rabbits — they liked all the willows that grew in the brooks. Father used to take me and Russell across the lake on the mud when the water was low, and learn us how to shoot with a .410 shotgun. He'd tell us "that's a good shot" so we'd learn to judge distance and when to shoot and how far the gun was good for. We used to hunt snipe, go over in the grass and the snipe would fly up and we'd shoot them; never got many — they were awful fast. We'd throw them in the same pot as the nansearies. Once in a while we'd get a bittern. Me and Jim Michelin was hunting one time. The bittern came over my head, coming further and further, and I was leaning back further and further for a shot and went "bang" and went right over the stern of the canoe. I couldn't see no sign of Jim but all at once I heard him blowing under the canoe; the canoe was turned bottom up and Jim was under it. It was a 12-gauge shotgun, and me not thinking about the kick; the old bittern just went on.

Grandfather's house at the Rapids was log, about 12 by 12. Edward Andrew has a cabin there now. Old Great-Grandfather John Montague built up there first; his house was about 16 by 20 or 24. I only ever saw the foundation of that one. I don't think he ever had a house here in North West River. Wilbert and me talked about it and we never knew him to have one here. Tom Blake and his family lived across the Rapids on the north side. I never saw Tom — he died before my time — but I remember his wife, Elizabeth. I remember her as an old woman living down here with her son Sid and his wife Alfreda.

When Grandfather and Grandmother got older, they lived down here. Grandfather was 75 when he died. Grandfather had Alzheimer's. We didn't know it then but now I know what it was. Some of us children would sleep down at their house with them, bring in wood and water and help them out. Those old people worked hard, even when they was older. Their three sons and their daughter and their families all lived close by so they had help.

After he got Alzheimer's, Grandfather went to his traps up in **the Springs** one time in the late fall and he got lost and we had to search for him. Leslie Michelin found him about four o'clock in the morning. He'd gone back further in the woods, away from the shore, and had a fire going; that was the last time he went in the woods by himself. He knowed he was lost. He told us the funny thing was that even when it was black dark, and he went to get a stick of wood to burn, every stick he come to was a good one, even though there was hardly a good stick of wood up there; it was just like they come right to him. He was a pretty religious man. I guess he thought something or someone was giving him the wood. He trapped all around Little Lake and around the Springs, up as far as Big Brook, when it was too far for him to go up above the Rapids. He had some more traps up in the brooks on the other side of Little Lake. It was hard for him and Grandmother with no government cheques like there is now.

Grandmother was a housewife; she used to hunt partridge and have rabbit snares around close. She was an awful woman for ice fishing — always fishing. Kate Austen [the subject of *Northern Nurse* by Elliott Merrick] and her used to go fishing together. All up and down the shore right here, between Uncle Harvey's and where my house is now, there were lots of trout. Tommy's daughter, Allison, is just like Grandmother, same size and everything, curly hair, looks just like her; loves fishing, too. My father had curly hair, too, and so did Tommy when he was young. I used to call him Willie Baikie 'cause Willie Baikie had awful curly hair, too. Ice fishing is a waste of time to me; it's best to wait until net time, put out your net, come ashore, and do your work and let the net do the fishing for you. I don't have the patience to wait for a fish to bite my hook.

There was an older woman who lived just past our house; we called her Gran Mackenzie; I never saw her husband, he was dead before my time; his name was Tom and he came here from Rigolet; she was a Learning from Sandwich Bay. Her husband went foolish in his later years. One time he harnessed his dogs to take Gran to the other end of town to visit Juddy and Maria Blake. He stopped halfway there and put up his tent and camped. The next day they went on, but he thought his dogs were getting too tired so he unharnessed them and put them on the komatik and he and Gran hauled the dogs the rest of the way. Gran lived in a two-storey house by herself, near John Michelin's. Us kids would help her out, mostly sawing and splitting and carrying wood in for her. People in the village brought her wood to her. She burned green wood and her house was always smoky. She paid us in candies that she kept upstairs, but they were so smoky tasting we could hardly eat them. She would visit at Grandmother and Grandfather's all day long, rocking in the rocking chair, but would go home at night.

Like most trappers' wives them days, my mother worked hard. She was a big part of our family's success. She sewed everything for us and lots of other people, made stuff for the craft shop, too. She used to get clothes from the Mission clothes store and cut it all down and make stuff for us. She sewed everything, even our peaked caps, and coats, and pants. She always had a hand-operated Singer sewing machine.

Mother used to help my father clean the sealskins, and we had a lot. She made all the sealskin boots and mitts. I remember our parents making sealskin boots together, all sewed with caribou sinew. They would make one each. My mother always cut out the sealskin boots and sometimes Father would take them up on the trapline and sew them in his spare time. If his clothes got tore or a button came off, he'd sew it up real good. He was always sewing with Mother and was right handy at that sort of stuff. She made some of our moccasins plus we got some moccasins from the Innu. When we went off trapping, we had at least two pairs of sealskin boots for first in the fall and then moccasins for later when the snow came. We wore **duffels** and knit socks inside them. We had rubber boots but never took them trapping. When we went off trapping in the fall, Mother had everything ready for us to go. She made it easy for us to go hunting and to be warm. Her house was spotless; she never sat down, always on the go, day and night. If she sat down, it was to sew or knit. When our father was away, Mother had to look after the dogs, too, cook their food and feed them in a big old tub, or feed them their seal meat: she'd cut it up and throw it around to them.

My mother never went anywhere. Aunt Mary and Aunt Florrie used to come to visit Mother. Uncle Piercy and Uncle Olin used to come up from Mulligan and stay at our house. Uncle Austin used to visit. My father was right in his glee when there were people around. I remember one time Father came back with a load of caribou from the Mealies [Mealy Mountains] and he had one thawed in the house. Uncle Piercy and Uncle Olin were visiting and they got to work and skinned the caribou right on the kitchen floor. They were all working at it and I was watching them, watching how they did it. My father gave them some meat to take with them.

I remember Morris and Bernard coming with Uncle Olin and Uncle Piercy [their fathers] one time and us kids set a net down the bank. We were too young to fire a gun but we had our pockets full of .22 cartridges and we'd put them on a rock and drop another rock on them, making a big bang. I remember there was a loon out there and we thought maybe we'd get him but they came out and made us stop. It was dangerous. Grandfather Montague used to have a net in front of his house and had an old rowboat there; we were always hauling the net, got loads of fish. All my young days centred around people coming and going, telling stories, and the house blue with [cigarette] smoke.

Sundays were cruising days; we put on our good clothes, went to church two or three times, and in between we'd go visiting, across the river to Uncle Mark Blake's or Uncle Selby and Aunt Pearl's; they were living over there, too. I remember Juddy and Maria walking up to Brian and Gladys's, especially in the spring when the ducks were on the go; Juddy would be out spying at the ducks, right excited.

Growing up we never thought about whether we were rich or poor. We never had much money. We had times when we were hungry. There was usually lots of meat and fish, although there were some poor years, but as children we never had much store-bought food. Mother always had a garden and grew potatoes, turnip, carrots, and beets. She kept hens, too, and we had our own eggs. I remember the old rooster calling in the mornings. She had about 10 or 12 hens and kept them in a little log tilt with a wire fence around it for them to run around in the summer. One time we went berry-picking in the fall and someone else was looking after them. When we came back, the weasels had killed them all. In the summer, us kids would take the wheelbarrow and go to the beach to get shells for the chickens to eat. The Grenfell Mission got people into trying different things like that. One time when we had no chickens, I remember keeping some puppies in the little tilt and wire pen.

In the fall, we had to go around town picking up cow manure to use for the gardens; we hated that. The Mission cows walked around town all summer and there was manure all over the place. We were some frightened of the old bull.

We had a storehouse down by the **landwash**, about 16 by 20 feet. Father would store flour there in the fall, about three 100-pound bags. The flour came in barrels at first, and later in white bags inside of **brin bags**. People used the white bags to make underwear and drawers out of. He'd also order big slabs of bacon; I remember those slabs hanging up in the storehouse. He loved his bacon and eggs for breakfast. Henry and Mary Michelin stayed in that storehouse one time. I remember Mother going in to the hospital to have babies; she was always at that, she had so many. Mary Michelin looked after us one time while Mother was in the hospital. I was awful lonesome for Mother.

Another time, when Leonard McNeil and his family came up looking for work on the Base, my father heard he was a good carpenter and he sent Pauline down to ask Leonard if he'd come up and help finish off our new house. They stayed in that storehouse while he was working at our house, put in the doors and windows. Leonard was awful handy at everything; he kept the old washing machines with a foot pedal going for the women. Leonard liked music, the old country and western music; he played a harp-type of thing with about 20 or 30 strings and had a gramophone, too.

We'd run out of berries in the spring, in March or April, and didn't have much variety in our food. I remember a few times we ate porridge twice a day. When our father was gone trapping, Mother would get a few rabbits close by, but sometimes it was pretty lean. In the spring, the store was low on supplies so even if you were a millionaire there was nothing to buy. We would run out of flour; that was the worst thing, or run out of butter and milk. We had **Klim** and, in later years, we had cans of Carnation milk. When we ran out of sugar, we used molasses to sweeten everything, including our tea. I remember Mother making bread out of table corn meal, which was filling; that was a different corn meal than what we used for the dogs. People used to go by dog team to Cartwright or Hopedale looking for food in the spring and they'd come here doing the same. We knew there would be no boat and no supplies until July.

Our father was a real go-getter so we did okay. He had good trapping and fishing places so if one place failed, he had the other. We had a good warm house for the time. Me and Russell worked hard, too, and helped the family. Father bought guns for me and Russell so we could hunt. He bought a gas-powered stationary wood engine from Nova Scotia to saw our own wood, and then me and Russell would take it around and hire on to saw wood for other people. We kept the money we made at that. They used the horse from the Mission to tow the engine around and then me or Russell would set it up. We were steady greasing it. We were paid by the

John Montague, wife Mary Goudie, and four children at North West River. Louie Montague's grandfather, Robert, is the child on the left. Taken 1887 by R.F. Holme. From Holme Collection, 1.02.35, Archives and Special Collections, Memorial University.

Top photo: Louie's paternal grandmother, Hannah (Michelin) Montague (left), and Edna Michelin (wife of John Michelin), circa 1940s, North West River. Photo courtesy of Lisa Michelin. Bottom photo: Louie's maternal grandmother, Jane Blake Chaulk. Photo courtesy of Judy Blake.

Abner Chaulk, Louie's maternal grandfather. Photo courtesy Judy Blake.

Louie's paternal grandfather, Robert Montague, North West River, circa 1950s. Photo courtesy Vera Best.

Louie's mother, Dulcie Chaulk Montague, playing her organ. Photo courtesy Vera Best.

Louie, North West River, circa 1947. Photo: Aunt Mary Montague.

Louie's father, John Montague, 1957, Moran Lake area. Photo: Don Huxter.

Ruth Andersen Montague, Louie's wife, with daughters Peggy and Diane, North West River, circa 1960. Photo courtesy Lisa Michelin.

Louie and Ruth's children, circa 2001. Top, left to right: Diane, Jeff, Terry; bottom, left to right: Brent, Janice, Peggy. Photo: Louie Montague.

Louie guiding at Frontier Hunting and Fishing Camp, Ashuanipi Lake, western Labrador, early 1960s. Photo courtesy Michelle Marcinkowska.

Aukie Montague (left) and Louie Montague, North West River. circa 1950s. Photo courtesy Lloyd Montague.

Louie on fiddle, Aukie on guitar, Goose Bay, 1983 Labrador Heritage Festival. Photo courtesy Elmer Lakata.

# Me an' Ockie an' Grampa

*Moi et Ockie et Grandpère*

A French translation of the first verse is included with this rollicking trappers' song.

*Austin and Louie Montague,*
*North West River*

1. Me an' Ockie an' Grampa,
We got our minds made up,
We're going to Kaipokok River,
If Grampa don't give up,
We're going in for beavers,
Otters and muskrat I think,
We'll set our traps along the beach,
And catch a scattered mink.

2. Now Grampa said to Louie,
I think we'll go and boil,
We'll take our grub and kettle,
And go aboard the Kyle,[1]
Grampa said unto the boss,
To see what he had to pay,
He gave the Captain sixteen rats,[2]
And headed out the bay.

*Repeat Verse 1*

[1] *an old CN coastal boat that plied the Labrador coast in the 1930s and 1940s*
[2] *rat is another name for a muskrat*

Moi et Ockie et Grandpère
Nous sommes du même avis
On va sur la Rivière Kaipokok
Si Grandpère est encore ici
On y va pour les castors
Les loutres, les rats musqués, je pense . . .
On va mettre vos pièges,
On va attraper un vision.

**Singable translation.*

Atuan Ashini: "Old Otwan, he was my father's best friend . . ." Courtesy Eleanor and Richard Leacock collection, circa 1950-51, taken at the mouth of Kenamu River.

Innu camp near Révillon Frères Trading Company building. Sheshatshiu, circa 1930. Monsignor E. O'Brien collection. Courtesy of *Them Days* Archives.

Man on dogsled, circa 1920 to 1945. O'Brien Collection, 2.07.003, Archives and Special Collections, Memorial University.

stick for cutting. We'd saw the wood down by the shore where it had been boomed home and then people would use the horse and a cart to haul the wood up to their house and split and pile it. Walter Goudie drove the horse. I remember Walter would say, "Back one step, back, back," and the horse would do what he said. Father ordered the wood engine through the HBC manager or Dr. Tony Paddon. Father paid cash for everything. I can never remember him being in debt.

The first big boat he had was a 28-foot open boat with an in-board motor, built in Nova Scotia; he paid eleven hundred dollars for it. Dr. Paddon or the HBC manager would arrange to send the money out to pay for these things. Later, he sold that boat to Cecil Blake and bought the HBC boat, the 44-footer. After chainsaws came around, Ellis Baikie bought the wood engine and took it to the Islands and I guess it's still there. Every spring we went to Three Mile Point and cut a thousand sticks of wood for the hospital; everybody did their share, like a sort of poll tax. We hauled the wood out to the shore and then the Mission took it home in the summer, either towed in **booms** or loaded in their **scow**. We did that for years and years, me and Russell and our father. Sometimes, we'd camp up there while we were working at wood. I remember Henry Michelin and Walter and Willie Goudie camping there doing the same thing. We chopped all the wood down and cut it up with an axe. In return, we'd get clothes from the Mission clothing store, or milk and eggs in the summer when they weren't needed for the Dorm kids.

Irene worked in the house with Mother. Me and Russell did the outside work. In January, Father would walk across the lake every day to cut wood so it was ready for me and Russell to haul out. We had a lot of wood to cut, split, and pile. That was our only source of heat. In our school years, we'd come home from school and work at wood and on weekends, we'd work at wood; we'd go in the wood path over across the lake [Little Lake] in March or so; take the dogs over in boat, take them in the wood path to haul the wood out to the water edge to be boomed home in August, then load the dogs in the boat and bring them home again. It was hard work, the komatik bogging down, taking dogs back and forth. Father made sure we worked. He wanted everything ready so he could go trapping and hunting. He always had enough wood for the next fall so he could get off trapping and hunting when he wanted to go.

That's why I love the outdoor life now; it's all I knew, all I heard about when I was growing up. People used to gather in houses in the evening, smoking and talking, drinking beer if there was any. Our house was a real gathering place; that's what got me interested in hunting; I couldn't wait to get out there. Uncle Stewart used to visit a lot. My father never drank when we were young but he made homebrew in later years or would buy beer. When he was gone away, my mother depended on us. I remember going to the store for Mother one time; everything was in bins and barrels and had to be measured out. I remember buying coal oil by the gallon, bringing it home in a special can. One time, she sent me to get rice and some other things and a hole came in the bag on the way home and I lost all the rice before I got home, a trail of rice all the way from the store.

Henry Blake had no sons of his own and used to like to take me around with him when I was little. I went with him lots of times. He had a beautiful motorboat. He didn't build it but he was always fixing it up, changing the cabin around. I went down with him one time to Edward's Island to get **rockweed** to use as fertilizer for the gardens. I was about eight years old at the time. It was a beautiful day in the spring, calm, not a cloud in the sky. We used a fork to put the rockweed in the boat and when we got our work done, we were sitting back on the island, looking around, lots of seals and wildlife around. Henry was rolling a cigarette for himself and he said that it was such a fine day that I should have a smoke, too. He rolled one for me and lighted it and passed it over and I sat back having the big smoke. It used to make me sick but I kept at it. I smoked a bit before that, rolled up birch leaves in brown paper, or sneaked some 'baccy [tobacco] from my father.

When I was 14, and been smoking a few years, all on the sly, I went off trapping with my father. I was kind of worried how I would get along with no smokes. We camped the first night up at **Watties**. The fire was burning, the kettle was boiled, and I was wanting a smoke bad, laid back in a brand new tent that Mother had made. He threw a brown paper bag over to me, full of cigarette papers and 'baccy; well, I was some happy. Later that night, he woke me up and said that the tent was half-burned from a spark from the stove. I looked up and all I could see was stars overhead.

In the fall, we used to take Innu up the Naskaupi to where the Red Wine River flowed into it, three or four loads of them, also some to the Poplars and where Paul Michelin's cabin is now at the mouth of the river, lots to the head of Grand Lake, Traverspine, and Sebaskashu. We took the people from Mulligan back home, too. They'd come up in rowboats in the fall to get their **fit out** because it froze up early down there, then we'd take them back with their supplies; that was Uncle Olin, Uncle Piercy, and Uncle Dan. We'd tow the rowboat back behind us; I would take my own rowboat for a lifeboat and to go ashore, 'cause you anchored the big motorboat out. I was doing that when I was 12 or 13, good fun, thought I was a man then, right big feeling, doing a man's work. One time you could take that old motorboat, loaded, through Shoal Tickle; it was very narrow and you had to slow right down, but you could get through. Now, you can't paddle a canoe through there. I remember one night, I left Mulligan in the evening after taking Uncle Piercy back; it was blowing a gale. I wasn't worrying about the wind, but I didn't go through Shoal Tickle; I kept outside Edward's Island and got home after dark. Father wasn't expecting me because of the wind and he wasn't pleased.

We never had no boyhood, us people; we went from a child straight to a man — we didn't know any different.

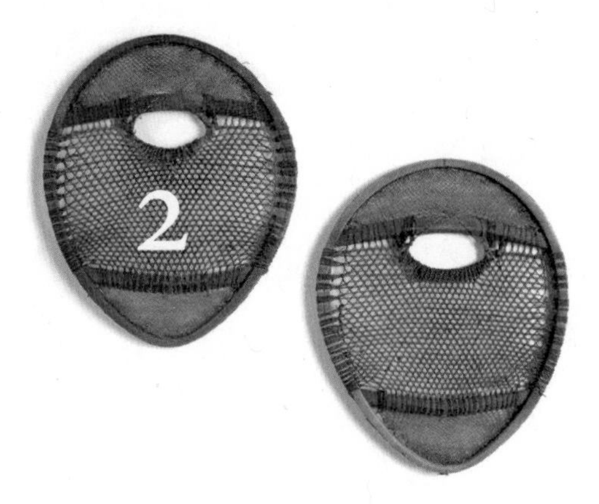

# FAMILY HISTORY

My people have been in Labrador since the late 1700s. Most of my people came from England or Scotland; landed on the Coast; married Aboriginal women, usually Inuit; and became trappers and fishermen. When it got crowded on the Coast, they moved inland because the trapping was good in here. They would still go back to the Coast in the summers to fish for salmon and cod and sell their catch commercially to traders who came to the Coast in the summers. Then, in the fall, they'd move back up here for trapping. They settled in the upper Lake Melville area in places like Pearl River, Mulligan, or North West Islands and eventually moved to North West River when the school and hospital were located here.

My parents were John and Dulcie [Chaulk] Montague. My father was born in Traverspine, across from Happy Valley on the Grand River. His parents were Robert and Hannah [Michelin] Montague. My great-grandfather, John Montague, born in 1858, came to Canada in 1872 from the Orkney Islands of Scotland to work for the HBC. He came to North West River as a labourer in 1874, according to the HBC journals. HBC men came here on five-year contracts. I believe he renewed his contract for another five years and then stayed on, married, and had a family. John married Mary Goudie;

her mother was a Cree who had married a Scotsman named Goudie in James Bay. John and Mary had Elizabeth [married Charlie Groves], John [drowned at Mud Lake], Robert [Grandfather], Rosella [married Jim Michelin], and William [burned in a North West River hospital fire]. After Mary [neé Goudie] died, John married one of Uncle Joe Michelin's daughters, Esther, an older sister of Hannah who later married his son, Robert. John and Esther had Kitty [moved to the US], Charlotte [raised by Mark Blake's family, married Holden], and Stewart [died young]. After John drowned, Esther married John McLeod and moved to Nova Scotia. I remember my grandfather talking with a Scottish accent like his father, John, and using some of the old words that he used to say. We found it awful funny sounding.

My great-grandfather, John Montague, didn't live long. He died at 42, drowned in the Gull Island Rapid on the Grand River in October 1902; they never found his body. From what I understand, the HBC used to have a fur-trading post in Petitsikapau, near the border of Quebec on the **Height of Land**, and they used to take supplies from North West River to there with what they called long boats. Seven men on shore with **tracking lines** would haul the long boat through the rapids and one steersman would stay in the boat. At the time of his death, my great-grandfather was the steersman and the nose stem came out of the boat in the strong rapid and nobody has seen him since. They threw a line right out to the boat but he jumped out on the wrong side of the boat. That's what Uncle Joe Blake said; and his son, John Blake, wrote about it in *Them Days*.

An English explorer named Holme hired my great-grandfather John and another man, Mr. Flett, to make a trip with him from North West River to the Grand Falls [now Churchill Falls] in 1887 and wrote about it in his book, *Some Things I Have Done*. They got as far as Winokapau but had to turn back on September 12 because they were running low on rations. In his book, he called him a "young and splendid man" and "a magnificent physical specimen" and said "no better companion could have been found for me." There are some wonderful pictures of old John Montague in Holme's book. Holme learned that John had drowned after corresponding with Elliott Merrick, author of *True North* and *Northern Nurse*.

My other great-grandfather on my father's side, Joe Michelin, was the son of Hannah [Brooks Mesher] and Mersai Michelin, a Métis trapper from Three Rivers, Quebec. Mersai trapped Kenemish and Grand River. He lived in Kenemish and later settled in Sebaskashu. Joe married Esther Lundrigan and had four children with her: Esther [second wife of John Montague], Ellen [married Malcolm McLean], an infant boy who died, and my grandmother, Hannah. [After Esther Lundrigan died, Joe married Mary Snow and had James, Susannah, Daniel, Robert, Charlotte, Stewart, Joseph Jr. (Job), Melvina, Emily, Mary, and Ruth.]

Robert and Hannah [Michelin] Montague had Austin, John, Murray [drowned], Harvey, Stewart [died young, unknown cause], and Mary [married Ike Rich]. Robert and Hannah first lived in Traverspine but moved to North West River, probably for their children to go to school. Austin [born 1904] and John [born 1905] were the two oldest and were born in Traverspine. Around the same time, other people were moving to North West River to be close to the school, HBC, and hospital. The hospital was in Mud Lake first but later moved to North West River.

Bob's Point, up in Traverspine River, is named after Grandfather Montague, always known to everyone as Uncle Bob. Robert and Lewis Michelin always told me that.

My father and Uncle Austin worked for the Grenfell Mission in Indian Harbour when they were little boys of eight or nine; they worked around the hospital when it was open in the summer getting wood, emptying slop buckets, and running errands. Uncle Austin used to work on the Mission boat that travelled back and forth between here and Indian Harbour. I think it was called the *Yale*. My father had TB [tuberculosis] when he was young and was in the hospital and then they kept him around the hospital to help out after he got better; he was kind of sickly when he was young, always had a bad stomach. When he was older they found out he had gallstones and took him to St. Anthony for an operation and then he was much better after that. I remember him bringing back two big bottles full of gallstones. I remember him getting a bad stomach on the trapline sometimes. Mother was a cook for the Grenfell Mission in Indian Harbour in the summers and then up here in North West River for the rest of the year. That was before she was married to my father.

My mother, Dulcie, was born a Chaulk in Pearl River, just below Mulligan. Her parents were Abner and Jane [Blake] Chaulk. The Blakes came to Battle Harbour from England as ship carpenters in the 1700s and made several trips back and forth to England before settling in Double Mer. They hunted and trapped in Double Mer and in summers, fished in the Rigolet area. I remember Grandmother Jane Chaulk very well. She and Aunt Kathleen moved to North West River after Grandfather died. I remember when she moved up here. She ran the laundry for the Grenfell Mission. It was in a log house and they lived in part of it. I was old enough to hunt geese and ducks with a shotgun, so I was probably 13 or 14 years old, and I would take some down to her, partridges, too. She loved that food, had to have that wild meat. I used to go over after school for a cup of tea; the laundry was right alongside the school. Grandfather Chaulk was long dead; I never saw him.

The Chaulks came from England to Newfoundland and then to Labrador from Tilt Cove, Green Bay, Newfoundland, not far from LaScie according to Aunt Edna Campbell's story in *Them Days* (Campbell, 1992). The family of brothers and sisters came to Labrador around 1860 and settled in Stag Bay near Makkovik for five years, according to an affidavit filed with the Privy Council; then they moved to Double Brook and stayed there for two or three years. Mother always said that when the Chaulk brothers settled in Stag Bay, two of the brothers went on further north and they never heard tell of them again. I asked Bernard Chaulk about that and he remembered his father, Uncle Piercy, telling him the same thing. Later the Chaulk brothers moved to Virginia Island in upper Lake Melville and then moved down the Bay to Pearl River in the early 1900s. Some years ago a cannonball was found on Virginia Island but we have no idea of the story behind it. Mother told us that when her family lived at Virginia Island there was a Goudie family lived there, too, and they had a goat.

There were also three or four sisters who came with the Chaulk brothers; their names were Dorcas [married William Sheppard], Amma, and Amy.

Amma married into the White family. Alexander Chaulk married Eliza Wolfrey and lived in Rigolet, where he died in 1911. The three brothers who came up the Bay were Amon, Abner, and Andrew. My mother's father was Abner. Abner and Andrew married sisters, the daughters of Mark Blake and Sarah Jane Oliver. Esther [married Andrew] and Jane [my grandmother] had a brother Joe who lived in Mud Lake. After Mark Blake died of a heart attack, Sarah Jane became Thomas Blake's third wife and had Uncle Bert [Blake], Aunt Flo [Baikie], and a girl named May.

Andrew's wife, Esther, died young. She was mentioned in **Arminius Young**'s book as being sick when Young visited the family at Pearl River in 1904. He promised to get "nourishment" for her when he went to Rigolet, which he did; but she died of TB at age 25 in 1905. Following her death, Andrew and their two sons, Russell and Olin, ages four and two, moved in with Abner and Jane. There had also been a girl, Flora, who died as an infant. I always thought Uncle Olin and Uncle Russell were Mother's brothers but she told me in later years they were her cousins.

One brother, Amon, never got married; he was crippled. He could get around but he couldn't go trapping. Mother told us that he worked around the homestead getting wood and doing all kinds of chores. Morris Chaulk's research showed that Amon was the head of the household and that the other brothers passed their furs over to him for selling, and that all the brothers shared their hunting and fishing harvest and revenue. Mother told me that Amon took trips to Newfoundland in the summer to buy supplies for the extended family and sometimes ordered food to come as far as Rigolet on the supply boats.

In the HBC journals, I read that Abner Chaulk came here to North West River to the HBC post from Mulligan; one date was April 26, 1890, when he came to pick up supplies (Davies, 1963). Abner and Andrew trapped at Mulligan and on the south shore of Lake Melville. Abner and Jane's children were Naomi [married Donald Baikie], Edna [married Dan Campbell], Dulcie [Mother], Pearl [married Selby Michelin], Myrtle [married Charlie White], Kathleen [married Edward Blake], Byron [married Maud Baikie], and Piercey [married Esther Campbell].

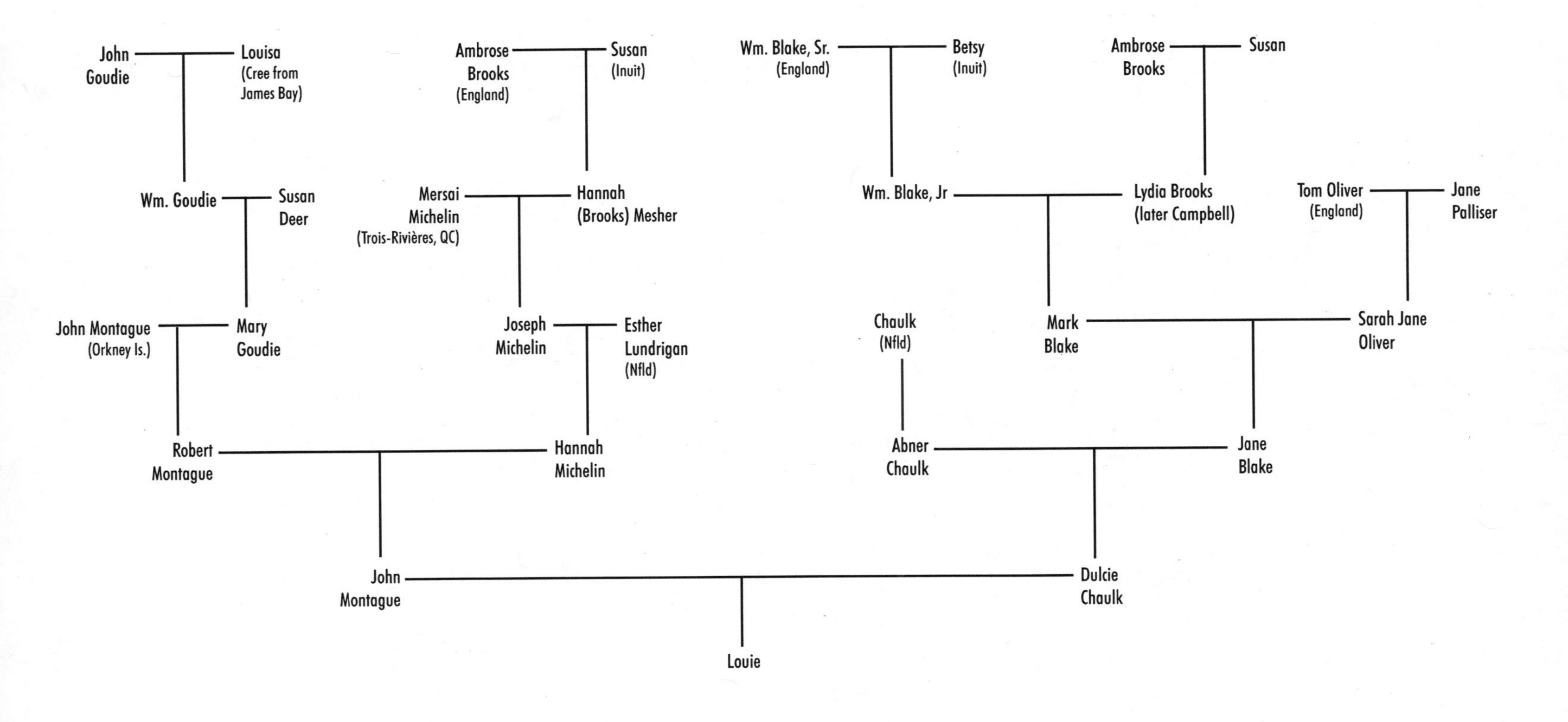


Figure 2: Louie Montague's family tree

My parents were married in February 1930 in the hospital at North West River. After Irene [married Wally Hepditch], the twins who died, Russell [married Minnie Beals], and me, my parents had Pauline [married Sam Andersen], Jane [married Wilson Gear], Vera [married Bob Best], Stewart [married Gwen Sheppard], Mike [married Pearl Simms], Tom [married Winnie Budgell], and Irving [married Carolyn Baikie (div.)].

I was my mother's biggest baby, over 11 pounds. I was born on Valentine's Day, 1935, and named David Llewellyn but was always called Louie. Russell and Stewart died a few years ago. Irene lives in Ontario. The rest of the family lives in North West River and Happy Valley-Goose Bay.

The Montagues weren't carpenters but on my mother's side, the Blakes were good carpenters. They were good woodworkers, boat builders, even built two-masted schooners, right here in the Bay. The Blakes could make anything out of wood and so could the McLeans. They built boats, too: rowboats, flats, and oars. I used to love watching Uncle Duncan McLean working with wood. He used to make play toys for us children. He used to make toy boats about two feet long; they were really beautiful. My father bought them for me and Russell to play with in the water.

When he was up the river on his trapline, on snowy days or bad days, Uncle Duncan was always busy making canoe paddles, axe handles, and snow shovels. When he came down in the winter, he would haul that stuff with his trapping gear and furs to the HBC. The HBC had a little corner of their store where he could leave it when he went on over to his home in Kenemish. They'd sell it for him and when he came back for supplies, he'd pick up his money.

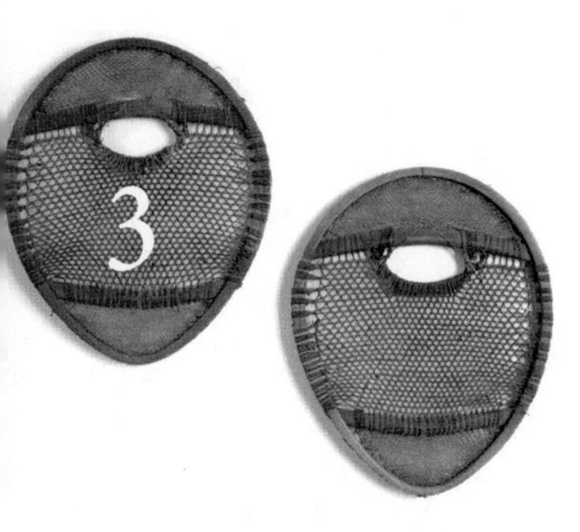


# EARLY TRAPPING YEARS

We went in the country twice, me and Russell. I don't know how old I was but I was still in school and so was Russell, because when we came back he had to go to school for two more weeks to finish it off and by law, you had to stay in school until you was 14, them days.

I remember our first trip well. We only saw Innu on our way in and Henry Michelin on our way out. The school was quarantined, closed down because of some kind of sickness. I can't understand why our father sent us way in the country like that; if we'd got sick ourselves, we had no medicine, not even a Band-Aid. I was probably 13 and Russell 14 when we made that trip. Father sent us in to **strike up** the traps in February; we gave up trapping early that year. If I remember right, we were gone 19 days, which was two days overdue for what Father figured. We went right in to Nipishish and one day on from there and back. I'd never been in there before but Russell had been in there that fall trapping with Father, so he knew the way; all we had was one dog and a sealskin sled.

We left here in February, me and Russell; we went up to Watties the first day, then the next day we got to the mouth of the Naskaupi River and met a big band of Innu coming out of the country after supplies and to sell their fur; we knew them all. There was a lot of them strung out along a snowshoe trail. We talked to them for a bit, then we went on. They were coming out to North West River. They talked to Father when they got home and told him they saw us. That was Joseph and Squasheen and old Otwan, Peter Jack, and Simon Pone; old Sapien was with them, too, and more besides, families and all, lots of small children. We had a good solid track from there to Red Wine River then.

The second day we went from Watties to the mouth of the Naskaupi River and five miles on to Henry Michelin's tilt where we stayed that night. Henry wasn't there; he was off checking traps. The next day we went on to our tilt at Red Wine River. I remember the going was good on the river and on Grand Lake; there was a lot of snow but it was blowed up hard in drifts. I enjoyed that trip. We thought we were grown men doing men's work.

That night going in the river to Henry Michelin's tilt was a real pretty moonlight night; a horned owl flew over us and he had a rabbit in his claws. He pitched out about halfway across the river from us to eat the rabbit and Russell shot at the horned owl, missed him but scared him, and he took off and left the rabbit so we had rabbit for supper that night. Henry Michelin was there when we came back out. We told Henry about our rabbit and the horned owl and he said jokingly that he often done that, but what he liked best was when them **partridge hawks** got a partridge; they would go and land in a tree and pick it [pluck the feathers] before they ate it; then after it was picked, he would shoot the hawk and take the partridge for himself; he waited until it was picked, then he shot the hawk.

It was really cold when we started on our cross-country trapline from the Red Wine River to Nipishish. It was the first time I remember hearing trees cracking with frost. We got a ways from the tilt and we come across a company of spruce partridge, killed 15 or 20; oh my, it was cold. You had to keep going; you couldn't stop when it was cold like that, just get to a cabin and boil the kettle. There'd be picked partridges and skinned rabbits hung up in the roof, right ready to throw in the pot; you would give them 15 minutes boiling and they were ready to eat. Then you'd pick or clean some of yours to leave there for the next time.

We didn't have much fur that trip; I remember in by our fourth tilt we had an otter and we had three or four mink, but no **cats** [lynx] although there was a lot of **sign**. I guess the traps were out of order because Father had been gone home since Christmas. We didn't know how to skin and clean the otter so we hauled it all the way from Nipishish; it was really heavy and we thought we'd have to haul it all the way home.

On the way home we met up again with Henry Michelin at his tilt on the Naskaupi. We told him we had an otter and didn't know how to skin it. He said that if we cut the wood for the night, he'd skin it for us, so we did. Henry had just got back from a day trip to his traps in Crooked River and he had a mink and a cat. We had cat meat for supper that night. We headed for home the next day; it took us two and a half days to walk home from Henry's cabin. Father was glad to see us. He had been very worried and was getting ready to leave the next morning to look for us. He had two dog teams lined up to go after us; Sid Blake was one of them. The reason we were two days late was because I had been in school and wasn't broke in to travelling like Russell, who had been on the trapline with our father all that fall. The first two days in from Red [Wine] River, we only made it as far as one tilt a day; we were up to our knees in snow and walking on snowshoes the whole time.

When myself and Russell were on that trip, he fell in a brook, right to the knee. It was bad cold and he froze his heel and walked on it all day, didn't know it was froze until that night. It was some sore; he had to walk on his toes the rest of the way in and all the way out. He was crippled bad.

I remember the second time I went in with Russell. We went up in company with Ross Baikie. We went to Watties the first night and then on to Henry Michelin's cabin; Ross left us at Berry Head Point to go to the head of Grand Lake; there was always a big hole of water at the mouth of the Naskaupi them days and you either had to go up in the Naskaupi to cross or outside and he crossed outside. I remember seeing him as far as my eyes could see, way out, going up across the lake hauling his sled.

Uncle Austin and Wilbert were up there in Nipishish to strike up their traps same as us. We went in to the fourth tilt and on the way back out to the river, in our second tilt, we heard all these people's voices after it was dark; it was Uncle Austin and Wilbert and Bill Goudie, three of them, and they were hauling their stuff out. Bill Goudie had a canoe. They brought their stuff out to the Red Wine tilt and then Bill and Uncle Austin went back in for some more trapping and Wilbert came on home with us. I remember that right well. It was pouring rain when we came home (in February). I remember there was a strong southeast wind. That was a long time ago, you know.

Like most boys around here in my time, I left school at 14 to go trapping with my father. I had been on the trapline with him a good bit before that and also with Russell, who knew the trapline as well. I trapped with my father the first two years and then went on my own after that. I'm not sure if it was the next year because nobody ever went trapping every year. It depended on the price of fur, the animals that were on the go, available work at home, lots of things. We knew if there were animals on the go; we learned from our fathers how to look for sign, and we would hear from other people travelling the country. In my time, some years the fur wasn't worth anything so you just didn't go trapping. I learned a lot about trapping from watching my father and grandfather, and Uncle Austin and others.

Me and my father got into it bad that first fall I was up with him. Between our second and third tilt there was a little deep pond; we went in and there was no snow on the ice and the ice wasn't very thick; we went in again after seven or eight days and there had been a big batch of snow after we come out. We were out in the middle of the pond and the next thing we knowed we were both down through the ice and the dog, too, and him with the sealskin sled. The dog got out quick and Father, too, but I didn't. I couldn't get out and I would be there yet but for my father. There was an axe and a gun tied to the sealskin and he got that and cut a long stick and poked that out to me. To this day I don't remember catching hold of the stick; I know I had snowshoes on but I wasn't carrying nothing; it was all on the sealskin. We were right close to our third tilt and my father made on a big fire right there and wringed out our clothes and got warmed up. Lucky, it wasn't very cold that day.

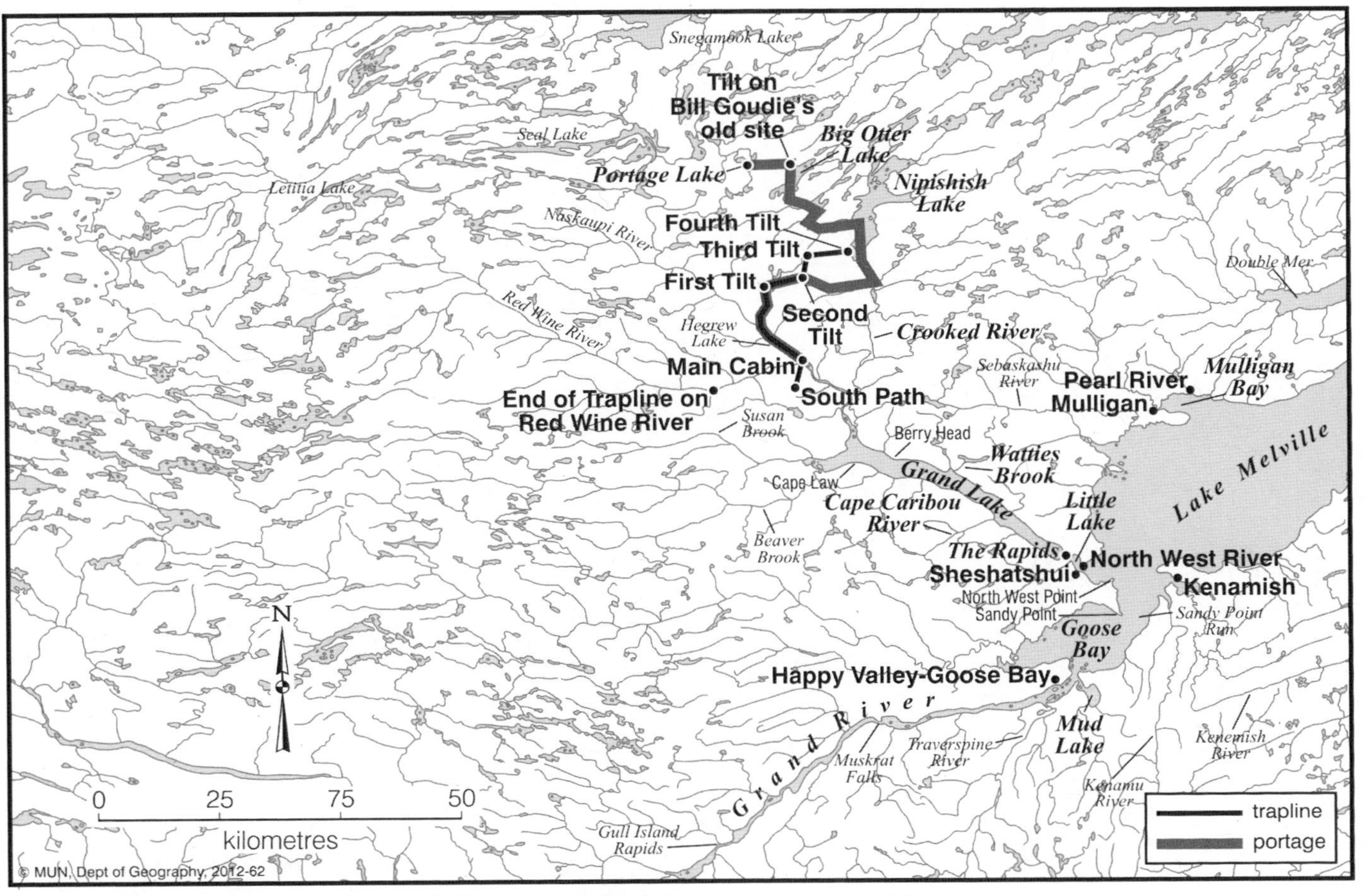


Figure 3: Upper Lake Melville and inland areas of frequent travel and use. Map courtesy of Charles Conway.

One year, in March, my father and me went up on dogsled to strike up our traps. We saw all these ducks dying on the ice and my father told me they were **tinkers** and **turres**. I didn't know what they were but he knew from being out around Rigolet and seeing them out there. Some of them were still a bit live, turned over on their sides and kicking but most were belly up, dead. There was a lot of them all along the Naskaupi. About a week before that we'd had a gale of northeast wind and snow, worst kind of storm; my father said they had got lost and blew in over the land. We didn't take any; we didn't need them and the dogs wouldn't eat them. I don't know if the wild animals would eat them but my experience has showed that the wild animals only eat the food they're used to; they won't go after a strange bird or animal. Out on the Coast, they tell me the foxes will eat seals but the inland animals won't because they're not used to them. I saw birds blow in here another time but there wasn't as many; same thing, it happened after another gale of **in wind**. **Bull birds** used to blow in here, too, from the Coast; they'd stay in the bit of open water that always stayed open in the North West River. They weren't much good to eat but we would shoot some.

For two or three years, my father ran a bit of trade goods at the Red Wine River for the HBC for the Innu when they came out of the country. We had flour, butter, sugar, tea, tobacco, salt pork, anything that could freeze and not spoil. We kept these supplies in wooden boxes in a tent supplied by the HBC. My father used to get 50 dollars a year from the HBC for doing that. The Innu would often come when we were on our cross-country trail and we'd come back and some of the food would be gone and some furs hung up. When the Innu came back to North West River, they would settle up with the HBC.

Our trapline was right on the Innu route between here and the Gulf of St. Lawrence. Some Innu used to travel back and forth every few years. They'd go out to the Gulf and stay the winter and then come back here. All the Innu here them days travelled back and forth to the Gulf of St. Lawrence and could talk French and Innu. They were awful good people to have around; they knowed how to do everything — they made all our toboggans and snowshoes and moccasins, and sewed and patched our clothes in the country. We shared our food with them; sometimes we'd come back home to get some more food for ourselves. They were really good people and I guess they found us good to have around; we never had no trouble.

In 1949, fur was a fairly good price and it was plentiful and I went trapping full time with my father. In the early 1950s, after two years with my father, I wanted my own trapline and I knew I was good for it. I knew the river trapline good, but not the inland part. My father's trapline was about 55 miles from here by boat or canoe. You couldn't go any farther in boat; you had to **portage** after that. One part of my father's trail went from the Red Wine River in to Nipishish, about 20 miles on the map, with three large hills; the route we took was probably 30 miles. I trapped in and out of there with my father. We'd be gone on that cross-country trapline for five days. We had four tilts and we would go to two a day in good going and then we had "a day on." That meant that we went one day further from our last tilt and the reason for that was to give our traps another night before we went back over them. The first traps had three or four nights for us to get more fur. If you asked any trapper them days how long his trapline was, he'd always say "so many tilts and a day on." That was the reason, so you had a better chance on your traps coming back. Sometimes we were six days if it was hard going. In the heavily wooded country where we trapped, you seldom got caught in weather because the trees protected you; usually you got caught only if there was a bad rainstorm.

We had a place in on the Red Wine River. That was one day, in and back again late the same evening. There was strong **tide** on the Red Wine; we had to use tracking lines going up, and then cross the river to the traps. It was good for tracking because every turn had a big long sand beach. We'd go all day and in the evening turn around to come back and come out in an hour. That was some good fun coming out. It wasn't rough water, just fast; there were some rocks so you had to keep [forward] motion on the canoe in order to steer it.

Then we had what we called the South Path. That was a hard day's walk. We'd paddle about a mile in the Red Wine and then take a path. That was lynx country. That's all we would get in there; got quite a few lynx in there. Sometimes you'd have a big batch of snow and the leg-hold traps we used them days would get snowed up and go out of order and wouldn't catch nothing. Then we had to get around as fast as we could to get them back in order. That was a big problem. But we always got some fur; there was always something.

The Naskaupi River valley was good lynx country. Other trappers did good there, too; there was Henry Michelin and Ellis Baikie in my time and lots of other people before my time. Ellis trapped Hegrew Lake, just above us on the Naskaupi, and he also had an inland trail and did quite a bit of trapping on the Naskaupi River. Henry Michelin was on the lower part of the Naskaupi. He was trapping that area on shares for the McLeans. Later on, my father bought that place from the McLeans. I trapped three or four years down there and built a cabin right on the foundation of the old McLean one where Henry had been. Old Malcolm McLean had that place and his son, Uncle Duncan McLean, trapped it and died at that cabin out to the mouth of the Naskaupi just before I started trapping, around 1948.

Bill Goudie owned a place on Big Otter Lake, quite a ways beyond Nipishish. Him and his brother Walter trapped in there. I went in there my first year of trapping on my own. I was 17 or 18. It was a long trip, twice as far as my father's place, hard getting there, too. There were two big lakes in there that were bad for wind and 18 or 19 other smaller lakes. It was 21 days from Red Wine River to Big Otter Lake. That 21 days was all portaging, carrying canoe and all in on the portage. I would make five trips along, average about six or seven miles a day; I had a heavy old soggy 16-foot canvas-covered wooden canoe made by the Innu. We used them all summer so they never dried out. I don't know how heavy it was, probably close to 100 pounds. Most of my **carries** were about 80 or 90 pounds after I got used to it, after a few days on the trail. I only did that twice on that portage.

Other years I waited until later in the year when the ponds were frozen up, then I didn't have to take a canoe. Then I'd take a dog and my sealskin. I'd go straight across country to Big Otter Lake, not on the portage. I knew the way. My father also had a dog and a sealskin sled and would go in to his fourth tilt checking traps. Every now and then I would come down to his fourth tilt at the end of his path, and he would have some food or a note left there for me.

Uncle Austin helped me build a tilt at Big Otter Lake on Bill Goudie's old foundation and I trapped from there. Uncle Austin went on in to Nipishish and I saw him a few times that fall. There was nothing left of Bill Goudie's tilt; he hadn't been in there for quite a while and couldn't trap in there any more so he gave it to me. I went to see him about it. The first year was on shares and then he told me it was mine; he didn't want anything for it. The last time he tried to go in there, he had all his stuff except the canoe carried in to the top of the Red Wine Portage hill and in the morning when it was time to go on, he couldn't carry his canoe so he had to carry all his stuff back out; my father wasn't up there that year so Bill stayed and trapped my father's trapping grounds that fall. In the winter after he sold his fur, he came up to our house to pay Father his third, his share. I think Father said it was eight dollars, but my father gave it right back to him. I remember it well.

I trapped Big Otter Lake area for four or five years. It was a long way inland and sometimes nobody else in there; I'd be gone three or four months and not a word from anybody, no radio or anything. Uncle Austin was in there the second year I went in and one other year, too. I used to go as far as Portage Lake, almost opposite Seal Lake to the north, but not down in the river valley. I used a tent up there; my big old husky dog would haul that on the sealskin. Big Otter Lake was never as good trapping as the Red Wine trapline.

That year when I came out at Christmastime, I came straight out to the river; it was just two days' travel if the going and weather was good, on snowshoes the whole time. The first time I came out straight, I came out with Uncle Austin and we came out to Father's second tilt and then came out on his trapline. We knew that country well.

Another year I came out with Uncle Austin. The food and game was awful scarce that year and the trapping was poor, a bad year for weather and snow. There was lots of beaver and we both had quite a few. I think I had 17 because I went at them quite hard when I seen there was nothing else; so we ate a lot of beaver meat and there was porcupine, but not much rabbit or partridge, only a chance one. When we headed home, we took enough beaver meat for the first two or three days. We were hauling heavy loads and we were a long time coming home, 11 days from Big Otter Lake to home; we only killed one partridge on the way home and that was our last night, up here at Big Point on Grand Lake; there was two and I had a shot and got one. We had lots of flour for **flummy** so we made a big pot of flour soup to make the most of our partridge. We were getting hungry on just bread every day and working like dogs.

It snowed continuously that year. Them 11 days coming home, it snowed all night every night and we had to put up a tent every evening. We never came out on my father's trapline where there was four tilts. We came straight across country and cut off a long walk; we still came out at Red Wine River; we hit the portage at our second tilt and then came out on our trapline. There was no trail. We beat a path every night with snowshoes so we could get a good start in the morning. We were getting so tired, Uncle Austin told me he wished we could come across a helicopter. I told him it wouldn't do us much good if we didn't know how to fly it anyway and he said he would sure give it a good try. I always thinks about that. He was always joking like that.

Me and Uncle Austin never saw nobody on that trip, not even Innu, until we got home. We got home Christmas Eve; everybody else was already down. My father had left a note for us at his cabin, knowing we were coming soon and he said he was pretty sure there was a canoe left at the mouth of the Naskaupi for us. My father and Ray Cooper and the Innu were just ahead of us. Uncle Austin and me had to walk all around the shore of Grand Lake because it wasn't froze up yet. We had no canoe or boat but my father and the Innu had canoes. They were ahead of us and a couple times we came to where they had boiled the kettle and the fire was still smoking but we never caught them. If there had been wind we would've caught them because that time of year with canoes in all that ice, they would've been slower.

Me and Uncle Austin had flown in that fall in a float plane and a couple fellows were supposed to leave a canoe at the mouth of the Naskaupi for us, but it wasn't there. When we came out, we poked around in the deep snow where it was supposed to be. They didn't go up that fall so we had to walk 40 miles around Grand Lake in around every nook and corner, hauling a sled each, on big old **bellycatters**, breaking through all the time. What a time we had. We left our loads at Big Point after our last night camping there and walked home light. Later when Grand Lake froze over, I went back with my dog team to get our stuff. I got into the ice bad with the dogs on that trip. I was only 17 or 18, so it was around 1953.

The plane cost $80 to take us in that fall; we were late going in so all the small lakes were froze up inside and already to your knees in snow. There was no use taking a canoe with us. That was late in October. We had to wait a few days to set mink traps 'cause they don't prime up until November 1st.

People sent letters to us when we were on the trapline. Sid Blake would bring them from North West River to his upper trap on Grand Lake and the Baikies would pick them up when they came to their lower trap next to Sid's. The Baikies would take the letters to the head of Grand Lake, and then Vivan [Baikie], in my time, would bring them from the head of Grand Lake when he went across country on his trapline to the Red Wine River and leave the mail at our upper trap, close to his lower trap. He'd hang it up in a tree in a canvas bag and we would pick it up on our next trip to our upper trap. Sometimes Vivan came on to Hegrew Lake to visit Ellis [his brother] and Ellis would drop the mail off to us. Sometimes we sent letters back the same way, usually only once in the fall and never in the winter because we didn't spend as long on the trapline then.

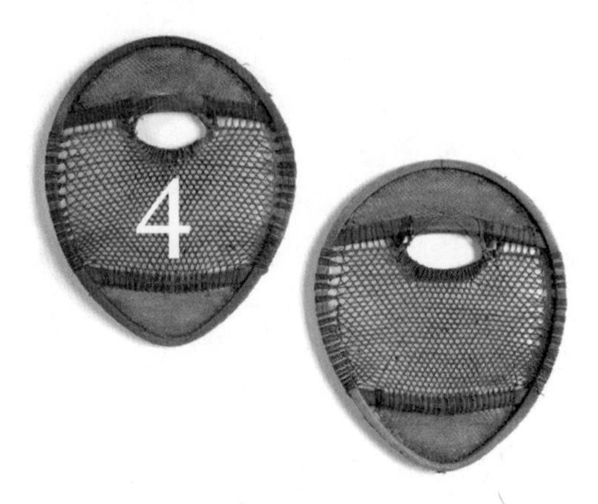

# MORE TRAPPING

Myself and Uncle Austin did a lot of trapping and prospecting together, and hunting around here. I've been with him a whole lot. I wish I'd asked him more questions but I never thought about it. I didn't know nothing about our great-grandfather but I never gave it a thought. I never even knew where he was from until I got older; then I started asking Uncle Austin questions. I found it awful interesting. I could have got a lot of information from Uncle Stewart Michelin too. I often think about that. Me and Uncle Stewart spent a lot of time together out in tent but I never asked him nothing. We used to talk a lot but everything he talked about was kind of a joke. I'm sorry I lost all that.

One night in to Big Otter Lake, my husky dog was going crazy on his chain; he was never like that before so I thought there was something going on. There was a gale of northeast wind and it was snowing and my dog was making noises. I untied him and brought him in the tilt but a husky dog can't stand the heat so he soon wanted to go out. After maybe 10 or 15 minutes I put him back out on the chain again. In the day I would let him run around, but not at night. Both myself and Uncle Austin was always wishing we'd get a caribou. We had seen some tracks, always going west, but we never saw any caribou. That night a band of 11 caribou came right along by my cabin, laid down in the snow, and slept there overnight. When I got up the next morning, it was tore right up with caribou tracks but I never saw them. Uncle Austin came up the next day and said, "Oh, boy, caribou meat for supper, I can see that," and I said, "No, boy, no caribou meat," just some track, some sign. Clear of that, everything else was scarce.

There were a lot of years we never went trapping for various reasons. If I didn't go up the Naskaupi, I trapped close around home, except for the two years I was in St. John's. That wasn't real trapping but I just had to trap, I liked it so well. I trapped in to McLean Lake for two years when I was working with forestry; I had a tent in there. I didn't go up Red Wine River those years. Saturday mornings, I'd take off in my car and drive up the North West River road and go in from there. I had a few traps set and caught two or three lynx and some beaver. Nobody else ever trapped in there that I know of. There was a trapline went in to the west of there that belonged to the Goudies; they used to do good with marten and mink in there before my time. Gordon Goudie used to go in across Little Lake and go across the marshes by Big Brook. He would be gone six or seven days on a round trip of his trapline; he had tilts in there and I saw one and some of his traps when we were in there firefighting one summer.

Coming home for Christmas after our fall trapping season, we got along okay if the weather and going was good on Grand Lake; that was the problem. Grand Lake was always partly open that time of year and you never knew what you were going to run into. I remember being held up one year for nine days right where Lloyd Montague has his cabin now. That was a real old trappers' camping place. There was me and my father and Henry Michelin. We could've walked home along the shore in three days but we were expecting the wind to die so we could take all our stuff home in canoe. We usually got home Christmas Day or the day after. That Grand Lake was the problem with its high bellycatters and the wind. You had to be careful going around a point in case the wind came up; then you had to find a cove to shelter out of the wind when you were paddling your canoe because there was very few places to land with a canoe. I broke up two canoes in my time on them bellycatters. I remember when it was mostly all bought cedar-strip canoes from the HBC, though the Innu used to make a lot of canoes, too.

I used to hunt geese in the fall. I remember going with the canoe on my shoulders and hearing the geese calling and throwing the canoe off so I could see the geese passing over. We'd go up the Naskaupi for a goose hunt in the fall and take our heavy trapping supplies in the big old motorboat. Then we'd come back home and haul up the motorboat for the winter, and go back up in canoe for the trapping season.

There were few black bears in the country then; we hardly saw any, just way back in the country on the berry patches. We didn't worry about the bears tearing up our stuff, not like now. The Innu were in the country and hunting them all the time. Bear was a big food item for them and for us, for their fat. I never saw a bear track on the Naskaupi then but now it's right tore up with them. We'd leave food supplies up on a scaffold, put stove pipes on the scaffold legs so the animals couldn't climb up. We never had a problem with bears. Now we have a resident population of bears and the big dump in Goose Bay that keeps the population up, and nobody killing them because you can't sell the fur. These days, bears can be dangerous because they associate humans with a supply of food. In my day we hunted them and if somebody got one, it was all the talk of the town for the winter because they were so scarce; what good fat and grease on them then. My mother and the other women were glad to have the grease for baking with. I've tried eating bear several times in these later years, but it's no good; maybe it's all in my head because I know they're living off the dumps. I wonder if I ate it and didn't know where it was from, if I would like it.

Over the years, I sometimes trapped on my grandfather's old place on the lower part of Grand Lake. While I was trapping there I was also getting food for my family, beaver, partridge, and rabbits. I loved trapping: never wasted a minute, off before daylight, back after dark. I got a nice bit of fur some years. I knew how to trap from watching my father and grandfather; that's all we heard talked about; we grew up with it.

Sometimes I brought Innu down from the Naskaupi River to North West River to get grub. They would come out to Red Wine River alone or with their families when they needed supplies; we shared some of our flour with them and they shared some meat with us. One time they told my father they'd give him some mink if he'd bring them down to North West River for supplies. We had an old rowboat with a 3-horsepower engine out at the mouth of the river, so he sent me down with them; that was sometime in December. There was a lot of broken-up pans of ice the full length of Grand Lake that time of year. I took them to North West River and brought them back again. I did that three or four times but I remember one time I couldn't get back to my traps. Hank Shouse had a small airplane with skis on it and I went to see him one evening and asked him if he could fly me in, and he said he would. The next day, we warmed up the plane and took off to Big Otter Lake at the end of my trapline. I had three traps at the end of the lake where a brook come in, and I had an otter in one trap, and on each side of the brook, I had a mink in each trap. He took them on home with him. Hank wondered how long I'd be and I told him no more than 10 days because all I had to do was turn around and come back out. I never slacked a bit, checked my traps, hauled a sled out to the river and walked the full length of Grand Lake, and I was home in five long days from Big Otter Lake, sometimes walking all night.

The portage by my cabin goes right across to the Gulf of St. Lawrence. Sometimes the Innu would go out to Seven Islands [Sept-Îles, Quebec] for the year and come back the next. That would be the same route they took north to Meshikamau. The portage was to avoid a large section of the Naskaupi River that was too rough to travel at that time of year. When travelling in the fall, everything was getting icy and freezing up, making it too hard to walk along the shore, and it was too rough for canoe. The portage avoided that part of the Naskaupi and came out on the river again at Seal Lake. Then they went on and portaged again, including around a couple falls, and on to Meshikamau. The furthest I ever walked in was to Portage Lake but I've been in to Seal Lake many times; I flew in there when I was prospecting. I trapped on the Naskaupi River as far in as Wapistan River some years.

As my father got older, I left my trapline at Big Otter Lake and came back to the Red Wine River trapline, our old trapline where I had started trapping. He was older and wasn't as strong as he used to be so he moved closer home on an old trapline further down the river. He told me he had to give it up; he couldn't do it any more. I trapped with him again in later years. I trapped and he stayed around and had a few traps around the cabin. He trapped closer to the mouth of the river at the place he bought from Gordon McLean; it was easier travel with no rough water.

I built seven tilts in my time on the Red Wine trapping grounds. One at Old Woman's Portage, two at Red Wine River, and four inland including the one at Big Otter Lake. I renewed everything on the Naskaupi River trapline including cutting trails to the traps when I took over. There were never tilts on the Red Wine River trapline; that was just a day trip in there and back.

Most of my working for wages was to get enough money to buy a gun or canoe to go trapping. It was all we needed. We lived with whatever was around us; we lived without money, not like now. One year, I never made enough to pay for my supplies, my 'baccy and stuff, but I always got along. In the summer, there was always work for various guiding or prospecting companies, geological surveys, diamond drilling and blasting. I did it all. I'd come home from my summer work in September and then I'd have all fall and winter for trapping. We were glad to get some money to buy our gear. Before we had snowmobiles we didn't need much money for trapping because there wasn't much expense. We had canoes that we used around home all summer for tending nets and travel; then we'd paddle up the Naskaupi in our canoes, use them all fall, leave them there when we came home at Christmas, and after our spring hunt, we'd bring our canoes home on a homemade **catamaran** to have ready for duck hunting in the spring. Sometimes we'd haul them ourselves and sometimes we'd take our dog team to haul them.

Our supplies that we needed for trapping was no more than what we would need if we stayed at home, some grub and 'baccy, same thing, same clothes, moccasins, snowshoes, guns and ammunition; it was all stuff we were using already. Now with snowmobiles there's a lot of expense; you could never trap enough these days to cover the expense and pay for it all, the machine, the maintenance and the gas; same with speedboats; you might cover more land with these machines but you're no further ahead; now any trapping is just a pleasure trip; you need a full-time job to pay for it. You can't make a living from it any more. We hunted most of our food that we ate on the trapline, even ate some of the animals that we trapped like beaver and lynx.

The first canoe I bought was a beautiful 16-foot chestnut canoe from the HBC; it cost about $300; a 12-gauge shotgun was about $70 them days. We wore a pair of long johns, a pair of pants and a pair of overalls over them, likely homemade, then a good heavy sweater and a canvas **dickie**; we were moving all the time, knew how to keep warm; when we left our tilt in the morning we kept moving the whole time; we stopped once a day to boil the kettle and have tea and a piece of flummy; it was mostly for the tea and a smoke and a break.

I never smoked going along; if you got an animal in the trap, it was the custom to sit down and have a smoke; you were so glad of the animal. If it was a good day and he was thawed, we'd probably skin it right there while we had a smoke, especially a small animal like a mink. When I was catching lynx, I could carry two in my pack, but if I caught a third one, I had to skin it to cut down on the weight. One lynx is about 35 pounds so I was good for two of them. Lynx stay live in a trap for a long time; you seldom got a dead lynx so they were always thawed and ready to skin. With animals like fox or beaver, you would skin them and leave the carcass by the trap to use later for bait. The best bait for fox is another fox.

I remember a hard trip in the country one time. I'll remember it if I live to be a thousand. We left Red Wine River and it was snowing and dirty, no forecast them days, no radio. It was dirty and wet with those old wet leaves and not much snow in the fall; every day it was pouring rain. We were laid up a day or two but coming out on top of Sunday Hill, the sky was starting to break up and I'll never forget how happy I was to see the sun. I think I was almost dead that trip, I couldn't take much more. I saw that sun come through and I said to myself "it's gonna clear," and then the wind came on to blow and our clothes froze on us but we weren't far from our second tilt. A big gale of westerly wind came and cleared the sky. It was really cold after that.

Another thing I saw up there one time, in December, we were at Red Wine River and there was a big southeast **mild** on for days and days, and all of a sudden one afternoon it cleared and the wind swung from the northwest and I never saw lightning and heard thunder like that in my life, in them hills, and never in December. I've seen it out here a couple times since, and once in the Mealies in January. We found it awful strange.

When December used to come, I would count the days to get home out of there. Not so much by myself, but when I was trapping with my father. There's nothing worse than someone giving orders to you all the time like that. When I was by myself, I didn't want to see nobody. I used to love trapping when I got by myself, everything was perfect. I liked to be my own boss, even when I didn't know nothing.

When the foxes were real fat, they were what we called "bold." They would go into the traps, no problem, but when they were real thin and poor, they were very timid and you couldn't get many. Even though they were starving to death or if they weren't feeding for some reason, they were hard to catch. All the trappers found that. Some years they were fat and you couldn't keep them out of the traps. It didn't matter what we used for bait; we used all kinds of everything, natural foods like partridge, rabbit, and fish — food they were used to.

Inland between our cabin and Nipishish, I've seen years when the foxes were really plentiful and we never got one, neither did Uncle Austin or Bill Goudie or the **Height of Landers**. They never used to get many foxes up there; the foxes were too frightened of everything, wouldn't go to the traps, but if they came to a river like the Grand River or Naskaupi River, they'd go to the traps right away. They would come to our tracks and circle around a couple times and run away back; they might do that four or five times, then make a big gallop and jump right over our tracks. How strange! It's something in them that we don't know about, don't know why they do it. We used to curse on them when they were fat and hard to clean. When they were poor and easy to clean, we would get very few and that was most likely in a snare and after a batch of snow; no other animals act like that.

In January when the weather was frosty and cold, the lynx wouldn't step on a trap. There was something in that metal; a rabbit would not step on that same trap, either; he'd go all around and eat everything but let it get milder and snow, and you'd get him right away. They won't go near wire snares when it's real cold, either.

Another thing I've seen, and it was talked about by all the old trappers and Uncle Austin got a story in *Them Days* (Montague, 1975) about it. The first so many years I was trapping, everyone was after mink; they were a high price. There used to be a lot in some places but I've seen them disappear overnight. Nobody knows where they went or what happened. Myself and Uncle Austin and my father were trapping Red Wine River to Nipishish; Uncle Austin was trapping Nipishish and way down to Moran Lake area at the lower end of Nipishish towards Postville and I was up Big Otter Lake, which is real good mink country. In the summer, myself and Uncle Austin had been prospecting in that same area and there were a lot of mink, just like the muskrats, a lot of them. That was the year myself and Uncle Austin flew in because the mink were so plentiful; we hired a plane, figured no trouble paying it off with all the mink we would trap, or so we thought. When it was all said and done at Christmastime, we all had four mink each, myself, my father, and Uncle Austin; we didn't even make enough to pay for our grub, let alone our airplane trip. They just disappeared.

We got in there in late October that year, around the twentieth, and there was a lot of mink around; we could see their tracks but in two weeks' time when it was time to set mink traps, they were all gone. And the four each we had were worth nothing; the fur was poor, matted and light brown; we were after the dark ones. I seen that happen two or three times; my father and Uncle Austin seen it lots of times; later, the mink came back again.

Lynx have gone through about three cycles that I remember and never came back; they're still not back. Naskaupi River was the best place in Labrador for lynx; there were more caught there between three trappers than was caught in all Labrador; now not a sign, not a print. No cats up there and no food supply such as rabbits. We don't know why.

Animals know a steel trap even though it's covered with leaves and everything. They won't step on it; they knows. You've got to bar them off in front of the trap house so they go in far enough and forget about that trap they just went over. The bait is buried about six inches in the ground so you make them dig for it. You get them that way. We use several pieces of bait and they go after the bait and dig it up. Another way to make trap houses is in a "V" shape and hang the meat up; the fox is looking up over the trap at the meat, and forgets about the trap, jumps for the bait and lands right in the trap.

Foxes are awful bad to eat one another. I don't know whether they kill the other one but if they come across another dead fox in a trap, they will eat it. Cats do that, too. They'll eat their own baby ones, not because they're hungry but for some other reason; it's their instinct. I've seen that a few times. Sometimes the mother gets in a snare and of course dies quick, maybe in an hour. On each occasion, the young ones ate the mother. When the mother one gets in the trap, she often has two young ones with her and she'll just kill the young ones with her but not to eat them. I guess Nature tells her they're not going to survive. Twice, I shot the young ones; they couldn't survive without the mother; they were only a year old but their fur was still valuable. You see all that kind of stuff when you trap, but we don't talk about it. It's all normal, nature. You have to learn the animals' ways.

There was a wolf on my trapline one time; he finally got in my trap, but took the picket and all and got away. Wildlife staff followed his track later. He ate a lot of lynx out of my traps, worth at the time about $300 each. He'd kill them live in the trap and eat them and tear up the fur. I came along in my canoe with lots of **slob** driving in the river and saw what I thought was a big dog in front of the door of my cabin; I was right happy because I thought I had company [people], but then realized it was a wolf.

For a few years there were lots of porcupine and then for about 15 years they were scarce and then they came back quite plentiful; now they're scarce again. I believe, me, there are so many cabins now and as porcupines are bad to eat paint and varnish and whatever they can get, I believe they poisoned themselves. They scrape the varnish off the wood and eat it; it's gotta do something to them. Years ago we never had that problem with our log cabins but we did have painted canoes, and sometimes we'd leave canoes in the country all winter, and they'd eat that painted canvas but not the bare canvas, like a tent. The same with paint and plywood with all the glue in it; whether it's painted or not, they'll eat it and chew it up to get the glue. You know Labrador is smeared with cabins now so there's lots for them to get at. There's no better meal for me than **swinged [singed] porcupine**.

When we went off trapping and took a young husky dog to haul our sealskin for the first time, we had to break him in. He was gonna be amongst the traps and snares so he had to learn. If he got in one he'd hurt his foot or run off and you'd never find him or your trap. We'd set a trap near our tilt, a #3 cat trap, **serve** the jaws all over with duffel so it wouldn't hurt his foot; then we'd set up a proper trap house with bait and wait until he got in it. He'd get in it almost right away; then we'd take a willow and switch him [hit lightly] a bit, tell him he did wrong, and then take him out. After that, he could run a mile ahead and lay down and wait by a trap but he'd never get in it again.

A dog wouldn't touch a live animal in a trap; they were too afraid. Sometimes they'd get too close to a lynx in a trap, especially if he was caught by the hind foot; lynx have a long reach, maybe 10 to 12 feet including the trap chain. My father told me one time about his dog that was going ahead of him in Red Wine River and at last he heard the dog screeching, never heard anything like it before. He'd been smelling around and got too close to the old lynx in the trap and the lynx had one paw on either side of the dog's head, holding him there, had him all bit up, his nose and everything. My father got there and the lynx still had the dog caught hold and he shot the lynx. I bet that old dog never got close to a lynx in a trap again.

I never saw a wolverine when I was trapping but I saw a track of one with a trap on his foot. My father and Ellis Baikie were trapping that year and I was in Big Otter Lake. On the way out to the Red Wine River when

I was about five or six miles from my father's tilt, I came across this strange track. At first I thought it was a porcupine because of the dragging sign. There was an awful lot of snow that year; I chased it for quite a while because I was hungry for porcupine; I found it strange that he just went on and on, never climbed a tree or anything. I never caught up with him so I came on out to my father's tilt. I told my father about the strange track and he told me that it was a wolverine with a trap on its foot and that it had been around his trapline for about two weeks, robbing his traps; everything that got in them, he'd take; he was heading for Nipishish but we never heard tell of him again.

When we came home Christmastime, we told Brian Michelin about it and he said he'd lost a trap to a wolverine on his place up at Sand Banks on the Grand River. It had pulled out the picket and broke the chain on the trap and got away. That's a long ways to travel from Grand River across country to Naskaupi River with a trap on his foot. Everybody was talking about it and no other trappers had lost one, so we knew where he came from.

Sometimes we'd lose a lynx if the chain was rotten or they pulled out the picket or something; they'd break it and go on with the trap on their foot. One year when we lost one, one of the Baikies came across country from the head of Grand Lake and came out Red Wine River and he told us he'd shot a lynx at the head of Grand Lake with a trap on his foot and he knew it wasn't his. If a lynx got away with a trap on his foot, he'd often stay close by and you'd get him. Sometimes he'd go a little ways and then climb a tree. You'd almost always get him. A fox would go on and on; you'd only get him if he hooked into something else.

I remember one time in Red Wine River, I came to a trap but it was gone, and out on the river I could see an old track where something had gone straight across the river a few days earlier. I went and took a look and when I got inside the willows I could see the track was pretty fresh. So I took off on my snowshoes with my gun and chased him for quite a ways; after about 20 minutes, I came to the place where I knew he had heard me. He started going with big old leaps; I started running after him and I came to the end of the track; there was a big old tree and on the ground underneath I could see brush and cones falling down. I looked up and old Mr. Lynx was looking down at me. I finished him off with my .22.

I had about four white foxes in my time, especially when the coloured foxes were plenty. If you had 60 or 70 coloured foxes, you might get one white one. I had one up at the Rapids one time and one close to my tilt another time. There used to be a lot of white foxes out on the Bay when we were seal hunting; they'd be eating the seals, the afterbirth and everything. There were always some dead newborn seals on the ice in the spring.

I saw a polar bear one time when I was seal hunting down the Bay; we thought it was a piece of ice but when we got closer and came across the tracks, we knew it had been a polar bear. I've heard of three polar bears in Grand Lake. That was a big story when I was young. Murdock Broomfield saw them when he was taking a load of supplies up for the Innu. Everybody knew about them and was afraid to go up the lake. Murdock had a 25/20 rifle but his father didn't want him to take it, didn't want him going after the bears, but he had to have that gun in case they tackled him. He came across three bears around Cape Caribou. There was no holding the dogs back; while they were going after the bears and going wild he was looking in his **grub box** for his cartridges. Come to find out, his father had taken the cartridges out the night before he left and he had none. The bears went in the woods and went on. That's all I ever heard of up that way.

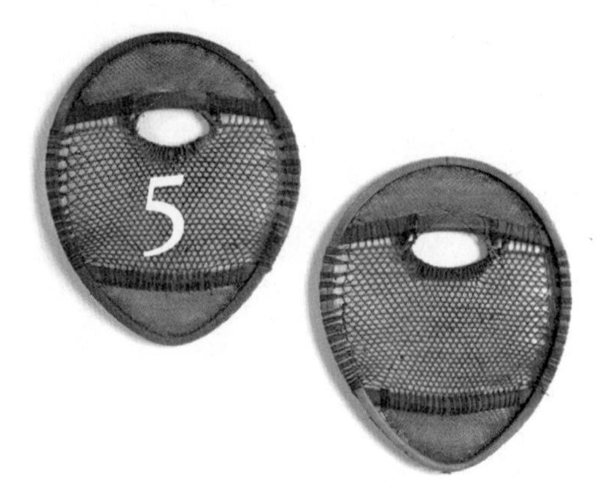

# NASKAUPI RIVER

The Naskaupi River was our living, our game, meat, berries, everything we needed to live. Our main tilt was at the mouth of the Red Wine River where it enters the Naskaupi. We trapped in different directions from there. We travelled by canoe first in the fall before the ice formed, used canoe on the river then walked cross country to our traps and carried everything. My father had a 44-foot motorboat with a cabin on it. We would take Innu up there in the fall when they were on their way into the country. They would have big loads, too big for their canoes, and they would hire us to take them as far as the Red Wine Portage; that was their portage. Some people called it the Innu Portage; some called it the Red Wine Portage, same thing. We took our heavy supplies up at the same time.

The Naskaupi River is a big river. I believe it's the third biggest one in Labrador. It's the same river that is called North West River here. The name North West came from the fur trading company that was here; it was called the North West fur trading post at one time. On old maps you'll see this whole river system, right to Lake Melville, called Naskaupi River. I read that the Innu name for the Red Wine River is Kamikuakamiu-shipu, which means "red water river." When there's a lot of runoff in the spring, the water can be real muddy and look reddish in colour so I guess that's where the name come from. The Innu name for the Naskaupi is Meshikamau-shipu, which refers to the lake that is its source.

The Naskaupi River comes from the biggest inland lake in Labrador, Meshikamau. It's the main source of the Naskaupi River. On the same river you have Seal Lake, a big lake; trappers from here went in there trapping. When dams were built at Orma Lake near Meshikamau [for the Upper Churchill power project], they dammed off our river to divert water into the Grand River. We had no idea about it but we noticed that the water in the river was getting shallow, causing it to freeze up real early. At first we thought it was just natural, due to a change in the weather. I remember my father and Ellis Baikie talking about the changes in the river and not knowing what was going on, but then we found out that there were dykes right on the Naskaupi River in by Meshikamau.

The only water we had left to come out through the Naskaupi was a few contributory streams coming in below the dams. Those were Wapistan River and North Pole Brook, a good-size brook. There was Shokamish Brook (that's the Innu name); then there was the biggest source, the Red Wine River, right where our cabin was. The problem was, there was such little water coming out that quite a few times we got caught with our canoes by early freeze-up in the river. It took a few years for the level to drop back as the new reservoir filled up; that was the Smallwood Reservoir, named after Joey Smallwood [Newfoundland premier].

We used to take our canoes out to Grand Lake because it always stayed open until New Year's. We would paddle out the Naskaupi to Grand Lake around the 12th or 15th of December. There was a ridge of ice along each side of the river but the middle was still open. There was a lot of slob and **ice driving** but we could do it. We'd usually wait until a mild day when there wasn't much ice driving and then paddle our canoes right out to the mouth of the Naskaupi [15 miles] and walk back on the ice. We would be planning to leave around the 20th or 22nd of December to come home for Christmas. We would walk down the Naskaupi then, get aboard our canoes, and give 'er for home.

After the dykes, everything changed. The Naskaupi would freeze by the 25th of October. In fact, one year I saw it froze on the 24th. The problem was, the ice would make strong enough so you couldn't use canoe but not strong enough to walk on because you still had a lot of mild weather at that time of year. The water levels also rose and fell so the ice didn't get strong for a long time. It was dangerous. That ruined the trapping in there. All the old traplines were made on water routes so you could get around to your traps by canoe. Eventually, I had to quit my fall trapping altogether. I gave it up. I could still trap after New Year's when Grand Lake froze up; I'd go up the river on dog team or later on snowmobile, but fall trapping is by far the best. In the winter you have big batches of snow, rising water, and it's really cold. The Upper Churchill power project was started in the 1960s and the official opening was in the early 1970s, but all the damage was done to the rivers before that. Right now, the Naskaupi River is useless for travel and trapping, and has been for some time.

I remember when we used to go up to our cabin in our 44-foot motorboat; now I have trouble getting through the river in my little speedboat with its outboard motor. Late in the fall I can't get through due to low water and because it's already froze up. I know one thing; I lost a lot from changes to the river, both livelihood and money. That river was everything to my family.

The change to the river mostly affected muskrat and beaver. I've seen beaver houses way up on the sides of the riverbanks; I see it even now. They build their houses in late summer or early fall when the water is high and then when fall comes on with lower water levels and brooks and rivers freezing up inside, the water falls back and their houses and **browse** are left high and dry, up on the side of the bank on dry mud. Sometimes they can stay there but a couple times I've seen that the ice froze down so far [because it was shallow water], that they couldn't get into their house or, if they were in their house, they couldn't get out of their house, so they perished.

The Red Wine River level has gone down, too. For about four miles up from the mouth, it was the same level as the Naskaupi so when the Naskaupi level went down, so did the Red Wine. Once you're in about four miles to where the Red Wine comes off the hills, it's the same as always. The Red Wine comes from a few small ponds and bogs so the dykes never affected it. The other rivers like the Wapistan, Salmon, and North Pole Brook still have the same amounts of water coming out through them because they come from higher land.

There are six rivers emptying into Grand Lake: Crooked, Naskaupi, Red Wine, Beaver, Susan, and Cape Caribou. There are large brooks at Watties and Cape Law. Some places they would call them rivers but we call them brooks. Beaver Brook is quite big. On some of the maps, they call them Beaver and Susan Rivers. Grand Lake is about 45 miles long, mostly east to west, right in line with the prevailing westerly wind. It can get really rough. We needed to have harbours to anchor in when travelling on Grand Lake but the old harbours we had for our boats have all filled in. We had harbours at Birchy Island, Burnt Point, and Cape Caribou on the south side, Watties Point and Berry Head on the north side. Those old motorboats were slow; they only went about six miles an hour so we had to make harbours if there was wind. When the speedboats came out, the old motorboats all disappeared; nobody wanted them any more. In a speedboat, a 16-foot speedboat, you didn't need a harbour. If you got caught in the wind, you just ran ashore, hauled it up, put up your tent and you were home free, plus you could travel a lot faster, 25 to 30 miles an hour. The harbours all filled in because there's not enough tide or current in Grand Lake now to carry the silt out. All the big clay banks and sand on the Naskaupi are falling into the river but there's not enough current left to carry it out, so it's gotta fill in. Same thing is happening in Little Lake, worse if anything; it's all filling in. The only way to get along in a speedboat now is in the channel right through the middle. It's all changing.

I always heard that before my time a family of McLeans was living near the mouth of the Naskaupi, and one of the boys, Sandy, went out hunting in canoe in the spring. There always was a hole of water at the mouth of the river where it never froze up all winter. That hole of water was good for ducks and geese in the springtime. This McLean boy went out to hunt in his canoe and while out there, the Naskaupi River busted out [i.e., a flash flood from ice breaking loose and freeing the river flow] and he had no time to make it ashore. Parts of the canoe were found later but I don't think he was ever found. That was the only fatal accident I ever heard of in that area. These days, there's no hole at the mouth of the Naskaupi because of less water coming out.

If you get a gale of northeasterly wind out in Lake Melville, you have salt water running up into Grand Lake. Since they dammed the Naskaupi, I've seen nets up around the Rapids with the tide carrying the buoys *up*; the water right boiling up through there. I never saw that happen before. There was never tide or salt water in Grand Lake. When there's a big gale of northeast wind, it fills up the Bay and pushes the water up here, and fills up Little Lake. It raises the water all the way up Grand Lake and even getting up close to my cabin at the Red Wine. I've tasted brackish water up as far as Three Mile Point in Grand Lake. When the wind and water falls back, then it's fresh again.

Trapping on Red Wine River has been affected, too, just like the Naskaupi. You can't run a boat or canoe up there now. One time, you'd have to use tracking line on your canoe to get up there because of the strong current running out; then you'd float back out with the current. Now it freezes up earlier than the Naskaupi. It only needs to go to 0°C and it freezes up just like a puddle. The last time I trapped in the fall on the Naskaupi was a while after my father was gone and he died in 1977.

I remember five or six years in a row when nobody trapped because the price of fur was no good. We were hunting and fishing around the lake here, maybe picking up a day or two of work here and there, but nobody went trapping. My father told me that at the end of the First World War, nobody trapped; the HBC wasn't buying any fur. He was born in 1905 and remembered that well. They put them all to work cutting pit props and railroad ties all around the Bay; after the wood was cut they never picked it up so people burned it. I think that was just to keep people busy. Long before Confederation that was, with people poor off.

There used to be a lot of geese on the Naskaupi when we were trapping up there. We didn't kill a lot because they were a big bird and we couldn't take many home but we always had some for Christmas and New Year's. Now it's no good for geese. The geese would start migrating south from Seal Lake about the 15th or 20th of October. The breeding place at Seal Lake and Thomas River is gone. Now the water is so shallow and freezes up so early, the geese have to get out of there early; they probably don't even nest there any more. It's just a puddle now that freezes early. The geese we used to get on Red Wine River were mostly the ones coming out from the breeding area around Seal Lake but that's all gone now since the dams. I talked to some travellers a few years ago and they saw a couple hundred geese in there but that was nothing; they used to be there by the thousands. There's a lot of bog area where they nest, also bog areas on Snegamook and Shipiskan, all over that country. Before the dams, I've seen geese so thick by my cabin that you couldn't sleep at night for them calling; now you might hear a rare goose.

When I was growing up and first hunting, we had very few geese around North West River in the spring but lots in the fall. There's more now in both the spring and the fall, and most years there are lots of geese around Lake Melville's shores.

The Naskaupi River is a good area for moose now. There were no moose in Labrador before the late 1960s and by the late 1970s we were seeing a lot. I used to see a lot when I was setting my traps. I was frightened of them a little. They used to hear me driving a picket or using my chainsaw and would come for a look. Best moose call there is, is a chainsaw or an outboard motor. When I had a moose licence I used to **steam** down the river and then turn around and go back; then they were all out for a look. They're really curious.

Moose drown a lot in the rivers in the fall when it's freezing up. They go out on the bad ice to try to cross the river and fall in and get swept right under the ice. Me and Lee Baikie saw one, one time, a big old bull moose. We tried to get him out but we could hardly lift his head. He was some big. His nose wasn't even froze yet and the hole of water wasn't even froze over yet. I've seen where they walked out on the ice and fell in. One time, there was five moose tracks on the sand across from my cabin; one had started across and got out in the middle and went down and the other four wouldn't try it and they went back. I've seen other places where the same thing happened. It happens a lot. I never heard tell of a caribou falling through the ice. They're lighter and they can spread their hooves out like snowshoes and bear up.

The caribou have been coming out on the Naskaupi for years now due to previous forest fires that made good food habitat. Forest fire is a good thing. We gotta have it. Without it there'd be no wildlife or berries. Fires way inland should always be left to burn unless there's people or property involved or commercial timber stands; then you have to do something about it.

The Innu would be up the river in the fall, catching partridge, rabbit, geese, and beaver. We would take them up there around the end of August. We'd put about three canoes on the boat or maybe tie two together and tow them along behind our motorboat. They always had big families with them. I remember one time we took old Michel to the head of Grand Lake. He went off hunting porcupine that evening and was gone until quite late at night. When he came back, he made homebrew. I remember him putting the water on the stove, mixing in the yeast and molasses and stirring and stirring. After a couple hours him and my father drank it and did they ever get drunk, or sick anyways. The Innu often had a boiler or pail of homebrew on the go, but it wasn't strong. I tasted it different times. It just made them sick and I guess they thought they were drunk.

The Innu up to the Red Wine River would build canoes, make snowshoes and clothing, and get ready for their cross-country travel. They had their sewing machines and used to take canvas and make new tents and clothing up there. When they went across country, they used to leave things like their sewing machines on a scaffold. It was a good place for birch and spruce, a good place for building canoes. They camped several places on the Naskaupi, like out at the mouth of the Naskaupi where Paul Michelin has his cabin now; there was a big encampment there where they made canoes and stuff; the Poplars was another popular camping place but the Red Wine was the biggest one of all.

HBC had an outpost about two miles inside the mouth of the Naskaupi

River. It was never operated in my time but I remember going down there berry-picking and there were old houses there, all fallen down. That place was called the Old Office; some people said it was haunted. A lot of people lived there, like Edward Michelin and his family; he's got two children buried there. Uncle Bert Blake lived there, too. Them days, people who trapped in that area took their whole families up with them in the fall to stay for the winter. There was no school in North West River and if they left their families here, there were about six or seven weeks before the ice was safe enough for travel, when they couldn't get down Grand Lake.

There were some families living at the head of Grand Lake, too. The men would travel around to their traplines from up there and then get back to their families easier. Some had houses by the old post; there was a house by the Crooked River, right where my brother Stewart's cabin is to. There were about three families used to live there; there was Allan Goudie (he looked for old Mr. **Hubbard**), and Uncle Duncan McLean, and later Henry Michelin and his family. Uncle Bert Blake spent a lot of time there but he and his brother Donald lived at the head of Grand Lake; they helped look for old Mr. Hubbard, too. They went and got Allan Goudie and Uncle Duncan to help them look for him. None of those families were living there in my memory.

There were families at the head of Grand Lake in my time, two Baikie families, Willie and Freeman and their families. Uncle Willie came across country from the head of Grand Lake and came out on the Red Wine River. When I was real small, when our family was living up there, Willie Baikie used to come up the Naskaupi; he always had candy for us kids; he stayed with us for a night and then went on up the Red Wine and we wouldn't see him again until he made his next round. We were always glad to see him. He was a good storyteller.

I found pieces of red bricks all around my tilt, don't know what they were used for or how they got there. There was red lipstick in tubes, too, and there were louse combs, cartridge shells, a lot of stuff, camping stuff. A lot of people used that portage over the years. Right by my tilt, the archaeologists and the Innu working with them found all kinds of things in later years.[1]

I learned a lot about carpentry from watching the Innu. They made everything they needed. They only had an axe and a crooked knife and sometimes a hand saw and buck saw. They made their own canoes, snowshoes, paddles, axe handles, snow shovels. They'd walk all day with a snow shovel, or if not that, a stick, for steadying themselves and trying the ice. The Innu were born working with wood. They'd knock down big old trees and split them with wedges. **On the last**, I saw a hand plane that the Innu used up Red Wine River. I still don't know how they got everything so smooth. They'd make their canoe timbers and soak them in the water for months, all tied together, right perfect. The timbers were tied together just the shape the canoe was going to be. They didn't have a mould, just used some pickets stuck up between some pegs. I wanted to build a canoe one time and I said I'd do it easier than the Innu; so I sent away for a book. Dear God, it would take me a lifetime to make a canoe the way they had it. The Innu would sit there with nothing and turn out a beautiful canoe.

When I started trapping with my father, sometimes we needed a canoe paddle or an axe handle or fur-stretching boards, and I started to try making them myself. I made a sled one time when I was on my own. I didn't know how but I had seen lots of sleds. I chopped down a good tamarack tree (or you could use birch). I shaped it out, worked and worked at it in bad weather with a little plane and a crooked knife. It was a little over seven feet long. I figured that would haul my stuff home at Christmas, my fur and everything.

1 Stephen Loring, an Arctic archaeologist with the Smithsonian Institution, in a personal e-mail (15 May 2012), explains some of what this dig uncovered: "In the fall of 1993 we (the Smithsonian's Arctic Studies Center and Innu Nation) conducted an archaeological excavation on the bank beside Louie's cabin. His cabin sits astride one end of an ancient traditional portage trail that went from the Naskaupi River to Seal Lake through a series of small lakes that avoided the treacherous rapids of the lower river. We did find lots of things besides louse combs and cartridges.... We didn't find any bricks at the Montague cabin site but we did uncover some downriver below the cabin site about three/four miles where there used to be a small forward post of the Hudson's Bay Company or ... a private fur trader.... Lipstick? I don't remember any [though we did find] pieces of red ochre (iron hematite)."

The more I worked at it, the more it looked like a sled. It was made in two pieces, two full-length staves, like the Innu made them. I put the cross bars on, tied them the way I remember the Innu had theirs, and then I had to curve the nose. I knew that was gonna be the problem. I had to have hot water or steam; I poured it on and curved the nose right easy. Every time I poured the hot water on, I'd bend it a little further. It got me and my stuff home, hauling with my one husky dog. I made that sled in to Big Otter Lake.

The other thing we used on the trapline was a catamaran, made with an axe or a buck saw if you had them. It was used to keep your load up out of the snow, like for hauling our canoe around in the fall. In the fall, we used canoes to get to our traps but when it froze up we couldn't paddle up against the ice driving in the river and we had to cross back and forth to get to our traps, so we used the catamaran to haul our canoes on the ice beside the river. The catamarans were about 10 inches high above the snow. The other thing the Innu used them for was to haul a sick person on. They were high enough to keep the person up out of the snow. They had real wide runners on them; they'd bear up good in the snow. They were made right on the trapline; you could make one in a day, a long day. You'd cut down a couple sticks, notch them out, smooth them out, leave a knob at either end of each runner, tie sticks across there with line, bore holes with a poker or an old gun barrel heated up in the fire. When you were finished, you left them where they were to. When you went back the next year, if they weren't there, you made another one. We never used them around town here. All this stuff came to us from the Innu.

I made all my own fur-stretching boards, made them of poplar — always lots of poplar around my tilt — I made them with an axe and then smoothed them out with a crooked knife or plane; in later years, I took sandpaper with me to do a good job. The Innu could smooth anything with a crooked knife. They were good at it. When you're making things like that, you don't just grab any old tree or piece of board; you look for a straight tree, pick it out of hundreds of trees. You look for one with straight grain; if it's not, you can't work with it. You can have small knots but not on the edges. You knew where there were the right kind of trees, growing straight. There were lots in that country. Spruce is pretty good; when it grows in the shade, the branches fall off, and there's not many knots. You gotta be careful with oars so the knots aren't close to the blade where the handle is narrow, because it weakens it, but it's okay if the knot is close to the top of the handle.

I saw where the Innu cut down big old white spruce, the biggest trees in the country, to make planks for their canoes. I also learned to make snowshoes, for my own use and [I] sold lots; I made lots of komatiks, boat oars, paddles, crooked knives, snow shovels, and **ulus**.

I made my first crooked knife a long time ago; I asked the Innu a few questions about them. You needed an axe file, heat it up red hot, put it on another axe if you had it or on a rock, and then beat one edge of it very thin. You needed another file to sharpen it. Then heat it up again just right, put the crook on the end, put the temper back in, and put a wooden handle on it. When I make them now, I remember exactly what they look like and how the Innu made them, the size, everything. I love to work with wood. I still do and I will till the day I die.

Seal Lake is on the Naskaupi River. First, you come to Little Seal Lake and then you go through narrows about a kilometre long and come to Big Seal Lake, a big long lake. They got their name from seals being seen in there. **Erlandson**, a clerk with the HBC, and four Indian guides travelled from Fort Chimo, Ungava Bay, to the post at North West River in 1834. While coming down a river that flows into Seal Lake, in June, he described many seals going up it. **A.P. Low** and others also reported seeing seals up there. I read about that in old HBC journals.

I trapped almost as far inland as Seal Islands on the Naskaupi River; that's about 70 miles from North West River and about 12 or 15 miles below Seal Lake. I've seen quite a lot of seals up that far. The seals were **doters and rangers** and they went in to Seal Lake in July, following the salmon and char that went in there to spawn. They were harbour hair seals and the doter is the mother and the ranger is the young one. They are fish eaters, eat trout and salmon. They have their young the first week of July, born all around Lake Melville and the Coast, but also born up the Naskaupi River. I saw a picture in *Them Days* (Grey, 2003) that a traveller had taken of a seal in Seal Lake long ago [1929]. By the time I was prospecting in Seal Lake, I never saw any seals in there.

I remember when our family used to go up the Naskaupi River to berry-pick in the fall and for a goose hunt, we would see lots of seals up there. As soon as we started into the Naskaupi River, I remember seeing 15 or 20 seals swimming ahead of our big old motorboat, frightened by the motor, I guess. They would swim ahead, not quite coming out of the water, jumping and going. My father never killed any because we didn't need them and the skins were worthless at that time.

We never used seal for bait for our traps. I guess the fur animals didn't know what seal meat was. I remember one year when I was trapping, there were a lot of foxes. I killed a ranger seal up by the Red Wine River and I said to myself, by God, I'm gonna clean her now with all this good bait and fat. That year the trappers on both sides of me caught lots of foxes and I never had one until later in the fall when the foxes got used to the bait. I was surprised because our old huskies would go clean crazy after seal. We used fish for bait and that was good for foxes even though they never caught fish themselves.

When I was trapping up there myself, I didn't see many seals although there were still a few. They were up there in the summer but we never went in the river in the summer — too many flies, and nothing to go for. The seals would come out to Lake Melville and out to the sea in late September or October. The Naskaupi used to be a good salmon river before they put them dams in there, so the seals were following the salmon for food. They didn't stay in the river in the wintertime although a few times I have seen seals on Grand Lake in the winter, lying on the ice when the weather warmed up in March. They got caught up there. I'd only see one seal at a time.

After I'd been trapping quite a few years, the government put a bounty on the doter and ranger seals, five dollars for the jawbone of the ranger and 10 dollars for the jawbone of the doter. Around the same time, their skins became a good price, around 60 dollars for the ranger and half that for the mother one. When the price was good like that, we started hunting them. Around the same time outboard motors came along and allowed us to travel further and faster and people started hunting them, and before long they were wiped right out. Today they're still scarce but they are coming back. The last five or 10 years, I've seen that type of seal around Little Lake again. They'll all come back again because nobody is killing them; there's no price for them now. Every year now I see a couple doters and rangers in the Naskaupi and here in Little Lake. I wonder how the dams affected them. I don't think that was ever studied.

There's a river that enters Seal Lake from the south, called Salmon River. When the Innu were in that country they would camp on this river for a short time to spear salmon in late October when the salmon were spawning. There might be a dozen places but I know of two where they speared salmon, good places with shallow water and gravel bottom; there's a fall above there and the salmon can't get over it. There's a pool right under the fall, full of every kind of fish. I've been to the place, seen their spears and their campsites. They would take lots of fish and dry them for winter use.

I never saw the Innu spear salmon but I know how they did it with a salmon spear. I've made salmon spears just to try it, as a craft item. They're different from the spears the Inuit use for char. The method was the same but I don't know that the Inuit used fire. The Innu had to spear them because salmon on a spawning ground won't bite a hook. In the night, the Innu would take a long stick, split the end, and put a piece of birchbark on the end and light it. The salmon would come to the light and the Innu could see them to spear them. They would do that from the bank of the river, stick the stick in the bank and lean it out over the water, or else use it from a canoe. The wooden handle of the salmon spear was about eight or nine feet long and they'd lean it out over the bow of the canoe. The spear itself was made of metal, usually made from an axe file.

I often wondered how the Upper Churchill project dams and the lower water levels on the Naskaupi River affected the salmon and their spawning, as they had to travel through the Naskaupi before they got to their spawning ground on the Salmon River. The dams for the power project wouldn't have affected the water levels in the Salmon River itself because it had a different source, but it sure would have an effect on their route to get there.

There used to be a lot of char running in through Little Lake and up the Naskaupi River. We'd catch them in the summer in our salmon nets and through the ice in the spring when they were running out with the slink salmon; the salmon wouldn't bite a hook but the char would go crazy after the hook. We used to catch a lot of char through the ice above the Rapids. I've seen my father catch a tubful to use for dog food. I never heard them called char; we called them "salt water trout." We also had sea trout that came in from the ocean. Char have become scarce now but some years we still get a lot of sea trout.

We used to get **ouananiche** in Seal Lake and on the Naskaupi, land-locked salmon they were. Other inland water fish were **maries**, whitefish, lake trout, brook trout, suckers, and pike or jackfish.

We all talk about the changes these days like salt water up in Grand Lake in the fall. Everything is different. I knew the waterways well at one time; now I have to learn it all over again but you can't learn it right because it's changing every year. Every year is a new year as regards to water and ice, like I was never there before. Grand Lake is a very deep lake; it's 45 miles long and will freeze up in January, usually within the first two weeks. My father tells a story in *Them Days* about rowing down Grand Lake on the 17th of January one year but that was unusual. Grand Lake freezes like water in a bucket and has to expand somewhere. Pressure cracks form on Grand Lake, sometimes heave up six or seven feet high in places, and push in 10 or 12 feet on the shoreline. These are dangerous places. You have to be very careful when travelling the lake. If you get a mild, like in the last couple weeks of March, some of these cracks open up; these pressure ridges or cracks will open up and get quite wide, dangerously wide, up to 15 feet, wide enough for a skidoo and komatik to go into. The ice is probably three feet thick but the cracks open up. You don't expect them to open until the end of March. When they close back up, they overlap and that's dangerous, too.

In 2010, we had one open up in January. We never heard tell of that before, opening up that early. It's very dangerous. There may be a skim of ice catch over the open water in between and make it look safe, especially if snow comes on it, but it's not. Sometimes, they'll split open at the shore and you have to go out around until you can find a place to cross. They split open right across the whole lake. They always happen in about the same place. The same thing happens on Nipishish and Big Otter Lake and even Lake Melville. They open and close several times with change in temperature and atmospheric pressure. It was always like that but it seems to be happening earlier now. You have to be awful careful when you're travelling around, always on the watch.

There's a headstone on Snegamook Lake, about 20 miles north of Seal Lake, where a fella died around 1928. I always wondered how that headstone got there. Peter Armitage told me that it's Louis Penashue's grandfather [Joseph Tshishenish]. **William Brooks Cabot** paid for the headstone and had it shipped to North West River. All of us prospectors saw it in there. Me and a geologist were paddling along one day and could hardly believe it. We thought about what a lot of work to get it in there but then read later in a book that [**Donald B.**] **MacMillan** flew it in around 1929 in his airplane.

My father took the painter Stephen Hamilton up the Naskaupi with him one fall [1941] and again in the spring when he went to strike up his traps (see Hamilton, 2002). When they were up the Red [Wine] River in the fall, it was freezing and thawing, got real mild after a cold spell, and the river looked ready to bust out. Father was pretty nervous and told Steve what might happen, and sure enough, they got up into the woods just in time to save their lives as it bust out. Just after that my father came down with the measles and was some glad he had Steve there to look out to him when he was sick. Hamilton painted a picture and gave it to my parents and it always hung in their home; it was there ever since I can remember but I don't remember seeing Hamilton even though he visited my parents a lot. I would have been pretty young. The picture was of the area by our upper trap on the Red [Wine] River, painted in the spring. Father said that Steve Hamilton told him he left his home and came here because he was getting too well known in his own home area.

One time up the Naskaupi I was using my chainsaw to cut pickets for beaver traps. It was making a big noise and all of a sudden I heard a big "bang"; it was a jet but I didn't know what it was at the time. I threw my chainsaw but I threw it the wrong way and it landed in the river. Me and [my wife] Ruth used to take our two younger boys up there [Jeff and Terry] and we had to give it up because they used to be crying and screeching, they got such a fright from the jets [NATO jets from Goose Bay on low-altitude training missions]. The jets came down the river from Seal Lake and Snegamook and through Hegrew Lake and around the bend there just above my cabin, and then right over my cabin. It was a terrible noise they made. I seen birch leaves flying from the force from the planes, and another time I saw a big **lop** on the water. It was early on a Saturday morning when me and Ruth were there, and we had to get off the river because of the force. Ruth went in the cabin and turned on the radio and heard that one had crashed coming in to land in Goose Bay. I wasn't surprised from the way they were flying. It was bad when you were in boat because you couldn't hear them coming [over the sound of your boat engine] until they were right over top of you and then you'd get an awful fright.

The Thevenets used to take Francis [Thevenet] by motorboat up the Red Wine River to his trapping area, and often stayed for a goose hunt. One time, we could hear them shooting and knew that they had got some geese. Later that day they came out of the Red Wine River and came over to our tilt. They gave us a meal of salt beef and vegetables; we were some glad of that. My father told them that our motorboat was leaking bad. We hauled the stern of the boat out of the water to get a look at it, and Henry [Thevenet] took the **stuffing box** apart and said he needed some graphite to fix it. All we knew about graphite was that it was in lead pencils so we gathered up what pencils we had and they had some too, and Henry took them apart and took the lead out and beat it up with a hammer and used it to pack the stuffing box and repaired it for us. When the Thevenets hunted geese and ducks in the spring, they would often throw some onto the shore in front of our houses for our families to use. They only ate the black ducks and would share out the rest. One time a plane crashed and the Thevenets got the engine out and made an ice boat. That spring they were going all around Little Lake here on the ice and in the water, with the big airplane engine going. They were some clever family.

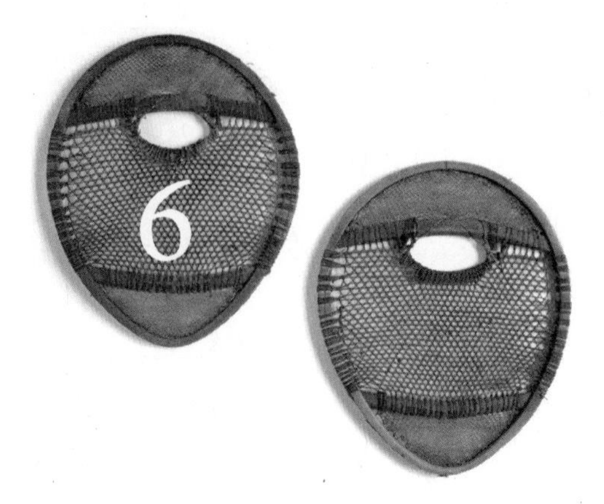


# WORKING ON THE BASE

I remember when the Goose Air Base started here, in 1940 or '41. I was about six years old; lots of excitement here, things we never saw or heard tell of before. The armed forces came here with big boats full of freight, oil tankers as well. They anchored out in Sandy Point Run; they couldn't get through the Narrows at Sandy Point. They off-loaded these big boats and tankers into smaller ones and brought the stuff into Goose Bay, a distance of 15 or 20 miles.

The first thing I remember was the big ships anchored off of North West River and the smaller boats coming here. The small boats were called "ducks" and they came ashore, hit the beach, and come right up on the land, landed right by the HBC store; they drove in around the buildings, and off-loaded quite a lot of stuff. Apparently they thought they were in the right place, where the Goose Air Base was going to be built.

They started right away, digging holes, right back of Uncle Stewart Michelin's house, in fact on his surveyed land. He checked into it to see what was going on; nobody had consulted him about his land or anything; nobody here knew why they were digging. I remember there were holes everywhere and them going right to it. Uncle Stewart told them they couldn't work there. Meanwhile these duck boats were going all over the place. Then they moved on after a few days up to Goose Bay, to the right place. There was an awful lot of excitement.

All the trappers were talking about the work coming, all the jobs and good pay at 35 cents an hour while they were used to 15 cents from the HBC or Grenfell Mission. At last the armed forces started hiring; people were coming from the length of the Labrador coast, coming by the thousands. They also came on the *Kyle* from Newfoundland, looking for work. I remember a couple times when the *Kyle* brought loads of people and they weren't allowed to land at the dock in Goose Bay until they were signed in. You couldn't just go to Goose Bay and jump off the boat and run all over the place. That happened to lots of people who didn't know any different. A lot of people got turned away, then went and got permission and got hired on. I remember a couple families who stayed on an island in the Grand River because they weren't allowed ashore. Some people that couldn't stay at Goose Bay came down here. I remember the *Kyle* unloading people down here several times and North West River people opened up the dance hall to give them a place to stay until they could get signed on for work.

The workers from Labrador built log cabins at Otter Creek, near the dock, and some brought their families. Otter Creek was where the dock was and where all the off-loading was going on; there was an awful lot of work as stevedores. They stayed there for a few years and then the armed forces gave them a place in what is now called Happy Valley.

I remember people coming from the Coast in the summer in their fishing boats and in winter by dog team. They came year-round for work. Many worked for a few years and went back home, back to their fishing and trapping; others stayed and settled here. That was an awful big change in people's lives, from fisherman and trapper to wage-earner making excellent money at 35 cents an hour. Uncle Jim Andersen from Makkovik told about him and some other fellers walking up here from Makkovik in the winter to get work and then walking back home in the spring before the ice thawed.

I think trapping was quite poor at that time. My father had a story in *Them Days* (Montague, 1993) and said a HBC manager told him that he bought furs from 90 trappers the year before the Base started, and the year after, only from five. Later, some people went back to their old places and tried a bit of trapping but it wasn't trusted to any more for a living. The long-distance trappers up to the Height of Land didn't go back except for Harvey Goudie and Harold Baikie. They were older and not working on the Base; they hired planes to take them in and bring them out. Really, that was the end of trapping as a living for most people; it was gone. Anybody could get a job and earn big money. My father never worked on the Base. He continued trapping and hunting and his salmon fishing, supplying the Air Base with fresh salmon. I don't think he ever worked in Goose Bay.

They hauled all the gravel for the Base from North West River, right at the end of the bridge across the river, where that pit is. They hauled it partly on a road they pushed through the bush and swamps, and partly on the ice, in gravel trucks. They had a cookhouse to feed the men and my father worked at that for a while, peeling potatoes. The boss told him that he should join the army because he threw away half his potatoes with the peel.

A year or so before all this activity, there were planes with surveyors flying around; in fact, one company set up here; it was called Skyways. They had these old Canso planes, like the Canso water bombers, that landed on the water. There were four of them anchored out on buoys in front of our place and John Michelin's. That was the survey crew. People knew that there was an air base being built; that was made public from the beginning. Everybody that could work went to work. We would take a bit of labour work if it was available. We were living sky high, making money. It was different than trapping when we had bad years, hungry years, everybody in debt to the HBC. Trapping was never steady; you never knew if you'd make any money even if you did the same amount of work. The HBC fitted us out and you paid up when you could. With the Base, there was a steady paycheque.

Men working on the Base stayed in Goose Bay; they lived in large army tents at first but soon after, the armed forces built big old barracks. They burned wood for heat and had a big crew supplying wood for that.

They cut wood around Goose River and had a big sawmill there. They cut saw logs to make lumber for hangars and barracks on the Canadian side.

When we were around 12 or 13, we would pile in a motorboat, or dog teams a couple times at Easter, and head to Goose Bay with whoever was going. We'd stay in the Valley with Uncle Ike and Aunt Mary Rich, Buck Michelin, or Alvin Michelin and hang around with our cousins and friends. We'd go to Henry's Point [the boat club road at the bottom of MOT (federal Ministry of Transport) hill] and hope to get a ride on a military truck, all covered in with canvas, that came to pick up workers. They'd take us up on Base to movies; we could get in with Uncle Ike on his pass card because he was working up there. I could never stay awake during a movie; I'd always fall asleep — still do. We couldn't wait to get some candy and ice cream from the PX store on Base. I especially remember how good the Coca-Cola tasted. Cigarettes were 10 cents a pack.

We'd see soldiers carrying guns, see the checkpoints going on Base; everything was new and exciting. There were thousands of airplanes landing and taking off: big planes with little ones surrounding them, the escorts. The little ones had wings that folded back, so they could fit them in the hangars. I loved watching the planes. We loved getting up there and having a look around. Frank and Doris Saunders had the first restaurant in the Valley that I remember, and we wanted to get there and get ice cream and candy. I don't remember eating a meal there; we didn't have enough money for that.

I had a couple jobs on Base. The first one was when I was 16; I worked at the mess hall in the pot room, cleaning pots, big change for me. I already had a few years of full-time trapping and there I was with a big old apron on going right to it, quite a change from a pair of dirty old overalls. I believe I got 80 dollars a month. I had our dog team up there and came home when I had days off. I remember working with Clarence Wolfrey at that job; he came up from Rigolet for work. I worked in the pot room for four or five months, then quit to go trapping.

A couple years later I had another job with the Canadian Armed Forces: me, Ossie Michelin, and Tom Broomfield all signed on the same morning as electrician helpers. I liked that job but after about six months, the birch leaves were turning yellow and everybody was talking about partridge and I quit again. After that they told me they couldn't hire me again because that was the second time I had quit. I told them that was okay; I didn't blame them.

I worked a couple times with contractors in the summer, doing roofing on them big old hangars; that was a heck of a poor job, hot in the summertime and working with that boiling tar, face all burned up. I was getting awful sick of it. One day I was sitting on a bucket up on the roof, waiting for a bucket of tar to come up on a winch. I would take the tar over to the roofer and take his empty bucket and send it back down. The boss man said, "Montague, what are you doing sitting there, there's a bucket of tar waiting for you over there." I told him, "That SOB can wait." I walked away; didn't care if I got my last cheque, but I did get it.

Before that, they were looking for a driver to drive a dump truck. They used slides to send the old roofing material down into the back of a dump truck to take to the dump. Don Preston had been driving but wasn't driving any more for some reason. The boss asked if anybody could drive and I said I could. The only thing I ever drove before that was dogs. He told me to drive the truck and I said I'd like to have Don Preston make a few trips with me to show me the way to the dump and all. So Don taught me how to drive right there. I drove for quite a while; I liked that. It was touchy at first. I had to drive that big truck over to Terminal Construction where they had a garage for fixing trucks, and back it in. I tried five or six times; buddy waving me in was getting cross, but I did it. I think that was all I worked on the Base. When I first went up to the Base to work, I stayed in the barracks, two to a room; unlimited food.

The place was full of soldiers, all armed. There were contractors working all over the place. They were really strict. You had to get signed in to the Base. There were two gates, one on the Canadian side and one on Loring Drive. They stopped everybody. Some civilians had passes that you had to show. One time something happened in the Middle East and the pilots were sitting in their jets and the staff brought their food out to them. They were ready to take off on a minute's notice.

There were all kinds of rumours about the Germans coming to take over; we had blackouts and heard about submarines off Rigolet. The air force went out and sunk a couple; the military were always afraid they'd get in through the Narrows at Rigolet but they had guns set up down there, watching out for them. I don't think the guns were ever used. There were all kinds of stories about Germans coming in to Lake Melville and Goose Bay but I don't think they ever did.

There were several sites built as part of the **DEW Line** system. One was at Big Point on the south side of Lake Melville, about 70 miles from here, and one on top of Sunday Hill in North West River; some on the Coast, too. Once the site was built at Big Point, we would often stay there on our way to the Mealy Mountains to go caribou hunting. In fact, I remember one year the caribou were right out among the buildings there. The site was never completed. They came up with something better, I guess.

Working on the site here in North West River, we got 80 cents an hour. They had a mess hall for their men to eat in, a cook and everything; they had big tents on top of plywood bases and they also had a barracks. Us local fellers would boil the kettle and eat outside but as fall was coming on, we wanted to eat inside in the warm. Somebody, I forget who it was, went around with a petition paper to get us into the mess hall, too. Uncle Joe Broomfield was worried we might get fired and us making such good wages. He'd worked for the HBC all his life for much less than that and he said he wasn't taking any chances on losing his good job. He said he didn't mind eating outdoors. We were all kind of frightened we might get fired but the strike never happened.

Most men in town were working on the site; there was Gordon Goudie, my father, Cyril Michelin, whoever wanted a job. We thought we were cleaning it then. The HBC opened the store late on Friday nights when we got paid so we could buy boots and parkas and warm clothes. We had lots of money to spend. The contractor had a **stake body truck** to run us back and forth. They'd pick us up in the mornings by the HBC store because that's all the road there was. They made the road in to Sunday Hill for that project. It was hard work, shovel and pick work; their men were proper riggers from **outside**. The contractor was Fraser-Brace.

I worked for Hank Shouse clearing the land for the site at North West Point. Lots of us fellers worked at that. That was in later years when the Americans built it as part of the DEW Line. We cleared all the land out there and burned the brush. One tower was 700 feet high. We worked up until Christmas and again after Christmas; we had our tents out there in that cove near Bottle Point, came home on weekends. After it froze, Hank used to run us back and forth in his big snow machine. A few fellas worked out there after it was done, Edward Blake, Jack Budgell, Jud Blake, Leonard McNeil, and others. They had a big mess hall, a bar, everything. We went out there and bought cigarettes and beer off the GIs. We used to sit in the club and watch TV. Henry Blake went out there to work. He wanted to buy a new gun and Uncle Stewart worked out there, too; he wanted to buy something, too. They were pretty old when they did that.

We used to boil the kettle outdoors and Uncle Stewart asked us if we knew how to clean a kettle outdoors over a fire. He made on a big fire and hung his kettle with no water in it over the fire on a kettle stick. He kind of forgot and then wondered where his kettle was; it was all melted and fell down in the fire. Uncle Stewart must've touched the stick on it. He laughed some hard. I saw it done the right way after that. All the black on the outside came off, and inside too, shiny as new. My father and Brian Michelin worked out there, too. We supplied our own food. It was fun, with everybody working together, making a few bucks.

The American armed forces brought in their own pigs and hens for food for the Base. When they didn't need them any more, they gave all the pigs away to local people but we didn't know how to look after them. They were some big old black and white pigs; we were kind of scared of them. They also had kennels of dog teams for survival work, for plane crashes. Hank Shouse, Eugene Cooper, and Tex Johnson looked after the dogs. Hank used to come down to my father's on the dogs. All three married local women and stayed here. A lot of the girls here married armed forces men and moved away. The American forces had a lot more people here than the Canadians. The Canadians were here a year or so before the Americans, I believe.

They had airplanes flying around pulling targets behind for target practice. We'd see and hear all that from down here. When they were flying to Europe, there'd be one big airplane with three fighters on each side. The sky was almost black with planes sometimes. They flew from here to Greenland and Iceland on the way to Europe. We knew the war was on; we had news after we got radios. We knew the enemy knew there was an air base here and we felt like we were kind of a target. It was kind of frightful. I was only young, but I remember. Grandfather used to get all the news on the radio. He heard that the Germans had airplanes with skis on them and they could land anywhere. He was some frightened. He was always afraid of war, maybe something he heard from his father. He said they could drop people from airplanes, too. That made him even more nervous. When they started bringing in movies, that gave us a look at another world. We didn't know anything about life outside of Labrador before them days.

As far as I'm concerned, the Base was the best thing that ever happened to Labrador; we had things; we saw things we'd heard about in the outside world; we had lots of food supplies year-round. Before that, we only had food come a couple times a year and we always ran out of food in the middle of winter. People had to go by dog team to Cartwright or Rigolet, sometimes as far as Hopedale, looking for flour or tea. There were times of barely surviving; but when the Base came and the stores, it was good. There was work whenever you wanted it; I just didn't want it. I wanted to be out roaming around the country. There was geological surveys and prospecting. Prospecting and survey work was good for us because we could work with them all summer, draw unemployment, and then go in the country trapping in the winter. That's where I wanted to be. We didn't know about unemployment insurance until the welfare officer told us about it. We used to play poker with him and I think he just wanted us to have more money so he could win it from us in a poker game!

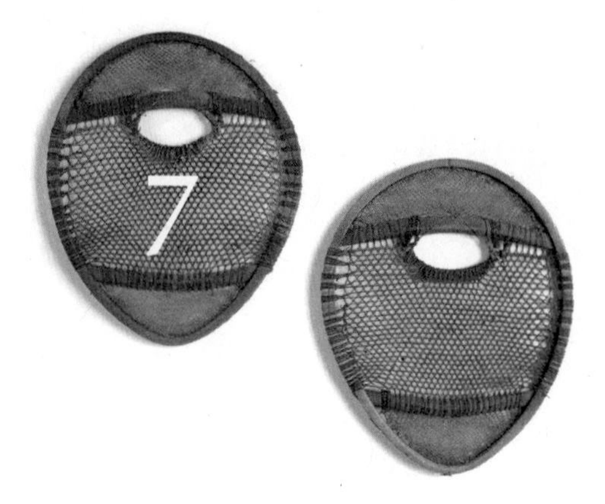


# OTHER JOBS

My first job with the government was with the provincial Department of Mines and Resources. I worked two summers with them as an assistant geologist. We travelled around in the country mapping the rock and looking for minerals.

I worked with **NALCO**, a government corporation, for one or two summers, doing geological surveys. Then, I went prospecting with Frobisher, then with **Brinex** for a few years. Brinex had a good uranium mineral showing near Makkovik, called Kitts Pond, and I worked as a driller underground, drilling for the blasters. I worked with Bill Michelin. We also drilled some deep holes and vents, right through hundreds of feet of rock. Me and Brian Michelin and Silas Baikie worked one year with Rio Tinto up in Letitia Lake, also Penute Ashini and Matthew Ben worked with us. Letitia Lake is up in the Seal Lake area. I had my dog team in there one spring from the end of March to the end of May. I used the dogs to haul the ore samples out from the hill to the lake and then they flew them out here. They were looking for beryllium, a very rich mineral. In June, the ice was gone off the lake and they took us and the dogs out by float plane.

There was a big herd of caribou in there and I went hunting for food for us and the dogs. Because it was late in the spring, I wanted to pick out a stag, but I shot a doe, a pregnant doe, worst thing I ever did in my life. We needed some for dog feed. I think that's the only time I fed caribou meat to my dogs, but we were out of dog feed. There must've been a thousand caribou there, right close to us. There were caribou being born there on the 27th of May that year. There's a long range of barren mountains in there where the caribou winter, but when it was time to calve, they moved across the lake and over to a bog area to have their young. I remember when we flew out of there, we flew over the bog and there were little caribou everywhere. After I went to work with Wildlife I told the biologist about it and we flew in there to have a look but there was nothing there. I guess a group of a larger herd just stayed there for a while and then rejoined the main herd.

Bill Baikie and I worked on an engineering project for Churchill Falls at Sona Lake, at the main camp; there were a couple hundred guys in there. One morning at breakfast, a guy wearing a white hard hat came in and said he wanted to see Louie Montague and Wilbert Baikie. We thought we were gonna be fired. We went with him to the office and he said he had a new job for us. He told us he had heard that we were trappers and had a lot of canoe experience, and that they were looking for canoe men. We were very happy to accept that job.

He told us we were going on the Atikonak River, and further west to the end of Ossokmanuan Lake. We'd never been there but they had maps. We had an engineer with us, Bert Kehoe, awful nice man but nervous of the woods and water. They told us they would take the canoe and the three of us and land us on the lower east end of Atikonak Lake and we'd leave from there to go on the river. There's a lot of rivers running into Atikonak River. We worked our way west to the railroad, right to the west end of Ossokmanuan Lake, about 30 or 40 miles long. It was awful rough. We had a 17-foot canoe for three of us; they brought in supplies for us. We were testing the bogs to see how far down the bedrock was. All day long, we would stop the canoe, go in on the bogs and drive a metal rod down and measure how far it was to the bedrock; it was mostly five or six feet, eight feet maximum. The engineer wrote it all down but they never did any more work on that project. What a good trip we had; lots of wildlife in there, caribou, ducks and geese, and the fish were teeming on Atikonak River because it hadn't been fished. There were a lot of caribou but we didn't hunt; we just fished enough to eat. What a pretty river!

We swamped the canoe one day. Kehoe was sitting in the middle, reading his notes, not paddling. All at once I saw a line across in front of me, something there but I couldn't make out what it was; it was a drop-off, a little falls; we went right over it and straight down, filled the canoe to the gunnels but it never sank; it was still floating. We floated on down the river with just our heads out. Bert told us that after that, he'd walk around any rapids. We told him that was better for us, too, less weight. We took turns in the stern, day for day; I was in the stern that day. Every time Bill and me met, right up until he died, we talked about that trip; it was a wonderful trip. We were on that trip for about six weeks, travelling slow because we were checking all the bogs.

We worked in there with Brinex getting ready for the Churchill Falls power project. Big DC-3s were coming in and landing on the ice on Sona Lake, bringing in barrels of fuel. We would take those barrels and haul them on komatiks over to the land, shovel off a place, and put them up on end. We never thought about what that project would do to the land and nobody ever explained what they were doing or asked us what we thought about it.

Me and Uncle Stewart, his son Ossie, and Leslie Michelin were in on Sandgirt Lake one spring, hauling gas up to the land off the ice where the planes had off-loaded it. We were working for Brinex and Leslie was the foreman. We stayed in an old weather station there. Somebody had died in the house and Uncle Stewart was some nervous; he heard noises at night; it was right on the Quebec-Labrador border. Me and Uncle Stewart almost got fired. One day the boss, Don Charles, came in and couldn't find me and Uncle Stewart. Leslie told him we were gone deer hunting; there'd been a plane in and they told us where they saw some deer tracks and Uncle Stewart wanted me to go with him for a hunt. That was the day after we got there. Don Charles told Leslie to tell us that if we did it again we were fired. Uncle Stewart found it some funny, first job in his life and he worked one day and almost got fired. To make it worse, when we got in there it wasn't caribou tracks at all, it was wolves. We cut holes in the ice right by our camp to get drinking water, and caught huge lake trout and pike right there.

Another spring, me and Uncle Austin and John Michelin were putting up tents all over the place for engineers; they were plywood floors and walls with a tent hauled over them. We had to shovel off five or six feet of snow in order to set up the tents; we cut firewood too, then we'd move on to another place. There would be three or four tents together. They were doing engineering studies for the Churchill Falls project. That was in the late 1950s or early '60s. We used to take a few traps with us and set them when we went in to a place like that. There were a couple plywood shacks in there and we stayed in one. We saw a track one time. John and Uncle Austin knew it was a marten track because they had trapped them in earlier years, but I'd never seen one before. John set a trap and in the night we heard the chain rattling and he had a marten. It had been living under the shack. That was the first time I saw a marten. We were catching minks in there, had quite a few.

We met up with some Quebec Innu and they had martens and a few mink. They wanted to trade with us because in Quebec the martens were protected and they couldn't sell them. So we traded our mink for their marten. Nobody in Labrador knew about protecting marten then.

Another time, I did diamond drilling, testing the hill for the Churchill Falls powerhouse; we drilled one place about a mile or so deep. That was with Shawinigan Engineering, all Frenchmen. They loved teaching me French, laughing at me when I tried to talk. Mealtimes, they'd name everything out on the table and get me to say it.

One year, me and John Michelin and Uncle Austin took three 18-foot canoes from Sona Lake out to the Big Hill portage and down to the Grand River. The engineers didn't know how we were going to do it but John knew about the portage. It took us three or four days to haul them out to the Big Hill portage, then lower them down. We made scaffolds and put them up when we got them to the river. I saw Wilfred Baikie's tilt in there; that was his trapping grounds.

I remember a couple summers when there was no work. The Base was pretty well built and there weren't as many jobs. After a while I got tired of being in the bush all the time. I wasn't married yet. I wanted to get out amongst the girls so I quit. Prospecting was almost finished by then, too. When I got married, I was mostly trapping in the winter, prospecting in the summer.

I guided for three years in western Labrador. I started in 1962 at Frontier Hunting and Fishing Camp on Ashuanipi Lake. It was a big camp with 22 guides and each guide would guide two people. It was a beautiful camp, all log cabins. Rex and Phyllis Klibbery owned it. Later, Rex left and just Phyllis was left running it. They hired four guides from here, all Montagues, me, Clayton, Wilbert, and Lester, and later in the summer, Brian and Jim Michelin. Some of the other guides were Innu from Pointe-Bleue on Lac St. John, Quebec, and some guides were from the Gander River area. The first year, we guided until the first of September and then stayed on to **clew up** for the winter. The next March, I got a call from Phyllis. She told me that her head guide from Gander River had died; he drowned on his wedding night, crossing the Bay in a boat, struck a piece of ice and tipped over. She asked me to be her chief guide for the coming summer. Some of us same ones went in again but not Clayton; he went to work at Churchill Falls that year.

The lodge covered a big area on Ashuanipi Lake. They had fly-out camps on Atikonak Lake, Joseph Lake, Kepments Lake, and on Chibougamou Lake. They had two Cessnas and we would fly out with two guests for five days to one of the other camps. We were a long ways out, 60 or 80 miles from the main camp. The rivers were really rough; we went through our paces in there, I tell you. We got along okay, only one incident when I was there; one guy put the anchor out from the stern of the boat and it dragged until it brought up solid and then went down, lost some camera equipment and other gear. Some of the people were old and there were women and children, too; it was a big responsibility.

We were out in the woods all day; you'd make on a fire, clean and fry the fish; some guests cooked their own. The Americans always rolled their fish in corn flake crumbs to fry, first time I saw that. They cooked fish chowder, too; I loved that. We always took our grub box and kettle with us. There were 14-foot fibreglass boats at the fly-in camps with a 12-horse-power West Bend motor, really good motors. The only trick was to change their shear pins from aluminum to a good strong steel nail. As long as I had one blade left on the propeller I'd get somewhere. They had bronze props on them; they were some strong. Going through those rapids, we couldn't afford to break a pin.

One time I had some fishermen out and they were getting pretty discouraged, no fish. Getting late one evening, before we came back to shore, I took them over to a beaver dam where a brook came out; there was a deep pool of water and it was full of suckers. They still couldn't catch any. They were trying every kind of hook and lure. When we got back, they told the others that they didn't catch any fish but it certainly wasn't the guide's fault, there were lots of fish there but they just weren't biting. I was some scared they'd jig one up and see his mouth and figure out there was no way that fish could take a fly.

The lake trout in there were really big, some were 40 pounds. The biggest one was 44 pounds. Mr. Moffatt of the moving company, an American, caught that one. He would sit all day and fish in the narrows, not get anything some days, just trawl back and forth, but he caught that big one. He was some excited. We got good tips in there, sometimes $500 for five days' fishing. If you done good with fishing, you got better tips. You worked like a dog, out on the water for 12 hours a day. They really trusted us. Tourists came from all over to Seven Islands, then boarded a DC-3 aircraft and landed on a gravel airstrip that had been built during construction of the railroad and now was used by the fish camp. The fish camp was close to the railway and close to the airstrip.

The next summer I went back again and while there I got a call from Edward Blake. I had applied for a job on the North West River cable car and he told me there was an opening if I wanted it. I wanted to get back home and so I took that job and left the camp even though they wanted me to stay on. I started working on the cable car in 1964. I worked with Junior Blake and Ron Lyall. We had one attendant in the car and one driving the machinery. We did maintenance and greased the cables, stood on top of the cable car and greased the track cables going across the river. It wasn't dangerous; we had straps holding us on. I went from working on the cable car one day to the provincial Department of Forestry and Wildlife the next day, in May 1966. I was hired for three months on forest fire patrol but when summer was up, they kept me on to do wildlife enforcement and patrols during the winter. I did that and then back on fire patrol the next summer, did that for years. I ended up working for the provincial government for 30 years altogether.

Working for Forestry and Wildlife was the most exciting job I had — everything was excitement. I worked for a while with fire patrol in summer and wildlife enforcement in the winter. Then in '68 I went to forestry school in St. John's for two years when I took a forest technology course. When I came back from school, I started to climb the ranks: I went from a forest ranger to a district ranger to a regional ranger; then I went to acting regional resource director for two years. I loved being out in the bush as part of my job, going on snowmobile and boat patrols. We prepared for fire season and stood by all summer for fires. We had a lot of fires. Later, they separated into two departments and I chose to stay with Forestry. Mike Parsons took over the wildlife job from me. When I left Forestry, I was a forest protection specialist; that was my job title. I enjoyed all my years with that department.

It was tough going to school in St. John's. I had left school when I was 14 with only Grade 7 or so, and I had been out of school for a long time. They helped us upgrade to Grade 11 in math, science, and English and quite a bit of algebra. Then we took all the forestry courses. I had an armful of books, couldn't even hold them all. I said to the boys at school, "If Ruth [my wife] could only see me now." But I studied hard. The course was at the College of Trades and Technology and I stayed in the Department of Fisheries dormitory in Pleasantville. They were teaching courses there for master mariners, fellows who would run the big oil tankers. There were some there from British Columbia. I got to know three of them really well and we had good fun together. They were my age. We used to play music on the weekends; I had a fiddle with me and other fellas had guitars. We'd get playing and stomping our feet. They moved us downstairs in the residence because the people underneath us complained about the noise, but they didn't make us stop. They allowed us older fellas to bring a little beer and have a few drinks on the weekend but we didn't do that much, never had the time, we were so busy studying. I knew a lot of people from the forestry department around the province; some were at the same course, and some from mines and energy; they invited me to their houses for supper and parties. They were awful good to me.

I really enjoyed learning and especially the forestry courses. The first morning the instructor said we were going to learn about botany. I never heard the word before and I asked the fella beside me what it was. "Flowers and plants and how they grow," he said, so then I understood. There was a lot on surveying timber lots and I did a lot of that work after; we learned scientific names of everything. We used to go out to Salmonier Line where they had a big prison farm and the prisoners were cutting wood there, so we went out to learn surveying timber lots. We learned all about wood: growing it, estimating, surveying, calculating cordage; that's where the math came in. In his book, Harry Paddon said forestry was a "jumble of math" — and so it was.

I was out to St. John's after that for more in-the-field training on surveying, some with the federal government. We also surveyed the timber on the Grand River, both sides up to the 400-foot contour mark, related to the dams they're planning now. It's all updated with technology now. Meanwhile Ruth was home with three small children [Diane, Peggy, Janice] and a fourth one [Brent] on the way. I got home Christmas and Easter each year; it was a big undertaking for her, too. I wanted to get ahead so I went after it and she supported me.

The summer between my two years in school, I worked with Forestry and Wildlife on a federal osprey survey in Labrador. This survey was related to the effect of DDT on the eggs of the osprey. In late August it was my turn to go on the helicopter with the biologist, Steve Wetmore. I can't remember the pilot's name. We were in a small bubble helicopter, a Hiller; the pilot was in the middle and us on either side. We flew south towards Minipi Lake about 50 miles south of Goose Bay. We checked a few osprey nests on the way out; when we came to another one, while looking at it, we were moving slow and I noticed the helicopter took a drop. I wasn't sure if the pilot did that deliberately but then he started putting out "mayday" calls and then I knew we were in trouble. We were going really slow and the helicopter wouldn't rise and here we were just barely over the treetops, and the whole hillside a solid timber stand.

The pilot continued to work the controls and the motor and call "mayday" but we didn't get any answer. We were then down below the treetops with the rotors still going and the brush flying as they clipped off the treetops. I knew we were really in trouble because there was no place to put down; it was solid big trees, black and white spruce, very thick and very big trees. That was the last thing I remember seeing. I must have blacked out.

The next thing I knew I was on the ground, couldn't see the helicopter but heard switches whining; I guess the pilot never shut them off. I took a few steps towards the sound and then I could see the helicopter right upside down. These helicopters had floats and the gas tanks were on each float; when the helicopter was upside down, the gas was leaking out but thankfully it never caught fire. The pilot was still in the helicopter but no sign of Steve. I helped the pilot get out and then I walked around, wondering where Steve was, and I heard him say, "On this side, Louie, on this side." When I walked around the chopper, he was pinned down but not in a bad place; he just couldn't back his way out, so I helped him get out. So there we were, up on the side of this big wooded hill, no place to look for us, like looking for a needle in a haystack. It was about two o'clock in the afternoon when we went down.

There was a pond we remembered seeing under the hill, and we decided to go down there, and hope it was big enough for a fixed-wing airplane to land. We [Forestry] had a Turbo Beaver at Otter Creek for the summer. We all had minor cuts from the glass in the bubble windows and were bleeding, and the pilot had hurt knees, I guess from the control column between his knees. However, he walked down to the lake by himself. The chopper had an Emergency Locator Transmitter (ELT) but we didn't know if it was working. We took it to the pond with us and hung it on a tree. We took an axe and food rations and kettle and fish hooks from the plane. Minipi Lake is known for its big trout and this pond led right into Minipi.

When we got to the lake, we figured it was big enough for the Beaver to land on. We bunked her down for the night. I knew there was a fish camp belonging to Ray Cooper on Little Minipi Lake; it was seven miles away according to our map. I told Steve that I was gonna walk to that camp; I had to go a mile or two and then hit the shore of Big Minipi and then just follow the shore. I didn't mind that it was getting dark; them days my eyes were as good as a hawk. When I got a little ways away, I heard Steve calling to me to come back. When I went back the pilot wasn't feeling well, blacking out, so I decided to wait until morning. I think he passed out a couple times, I don't right remember, so we bivouacked for the night.

The heavy woods went right to the edge of the pond but the trees were smaller by the pond. I went to work and cleared out a place in the trees big enough for a helicopter to land in case they sent one. I threw the brush and trees out in the water. In the meantime, we caught some big trout so we had a fine feed of roasted trout.

About two in the morning, we heard an airplane. By this time it was raining and foggy but not cold. This airplane came right over our fire real low, and circled around us three times, so we figured the ELT was working. We found out later that it was an armed forces plane from McGuire Air Force Base coming in to Goose Bay with a load of supplies; it was a big, big plane. We knew we were found and we knew all we had to do was sit there. Within a couple hours, other planes came in and dropped flares in the lake the rest of the night, kept it lighted right up. I think they do that in case people panic. I'd got a lot of wood in the evening so we kept the fire going all night.

The morning was real foggy but at last we heard our Turbo Beaver. It could find our beacon but couldn't find us. They had to go back to Goose Bay to refuel; the next time they found us but went on to Ray Cooper's camp. The pilot found the lake too small to land on with his crowd of doctors and helpers so he dropped them off at the camp and came back for us by himself. He landed on the lake and could only take one person at a time. It was only a hop over to the camp so it didn't take him long to whip us out of there. The pilot went first, then Steve, then me. They checked us all out there. There was staff at the camp, too, I think. We went back to Goose Bay and that was it. Everybody was glad to see us. They thought we had it. The plane that came from McGuire said they had seen the fire and knew someone was alive but they said the helicopter was out in the water but that was the brush out in the water that they saw, a good guess.

I never heard what was the cause but the pilot told me that he found the helicopter awful light. He had trained on that type but had been flying big helicopters off navy ships. He'd just come in to fly these and he found them awful light. He was leaving the armed forces and taking up bush flying. I never heard tell of him since. I went back in the same evening with MOT people in a DC-3 to look for the chopper. It was awful hard to see because it was directly down in a hole.

I think the reason we were saved was because we were still going forward and that momentum pushed or bent those big trees down, pushed them forward, out by their roots, and they caught up in the other trees, and we eventually stopped because we were going so slow and then just fell over upside down. We didn't turn over up in the air. We came down real easy. The pilot was working the controls but they were useless. I remember hauling my seat belt tight when we were going down. I had lots of time to think going down. I was scared. The pilot told us at the fire that night that he thought he'd been hovering too high for the speed he had and then went into a stall. I heard later they never found the tail rotor. I know the helicopter spun around a few times before it went into the trees. The three of us had to write a report and they were all different.

Another summer, around 1976 or '77, there were huge fires in the

Port Hope Simpson and Charlottetown area, in behind Parke Lake and right out to the Coast. That was the biggest and fiercest fire I ever saw in my life. There was a big crowd fighting the fire, locals and between one and two hundred men from Goose Bay area. There was high wind and the fire spread across the treetops. Inland on some lakes we had tent camps that we were servicing from helicopters. We had two Jet Rangers [helicopters]. One morning when we were doing mop-up after the fire, it was really foggy and with the smoke, it was like flying in soup. We took off, both choppers, flying quite low, going inland to the camps. We were together at first, one ahead of the other, but then we lost sight of the other one.

I was flying with a pilot who was IFR [instrument flight rules]-trained but the other pilot wasn't. We went way up to get above the fog and smoke until we got further inland. When we went up, we had no more radio contact with the other chopper; we were flying very high and couldn't find the camps and our fuel was getting low, so we had to come down. The pilot told me to look for treetops and let him know when I saw them. At last we saw them but there was no place to land. We'd passed over a bog but when we turned around to come back, we couldn't see it any more. He said we'd go up again and hope to get out of the fog. After five or 10 minutes, he said we had to come down and land, that we were almost out of gas. We settled down, down, down, looking hard, and then all I could see was water flying from the wind from the blades; we were over water; that was okay because the chopper was on pontoons; we could see the shoreline and headed for shore. When we got ashore, we had radio contact but we couldn't tell them where we were; we didn't know and couldn't see the shape of the lake, couldn't give them a description. But nothing could come in anyways in that fog and smoke. The other fellas had landed on a bog soon after we lost sight of them. Another chopper had to come and service us both, bringing fuel. I was never so scared in my life when the pilot said we had to land that last time, no matter where we were. No wonder we couldn't see any trees that time, we were out over the middle of a big, big lake. Everything worked out okay.

One September when I was working with Forestry, Bernard Chaulk and Silas Baikie had gone down the Bay to Valley's Bight on patrol and didn't return as expected. They had a radio and we had talked to them down there but we lost contact and there was bad weather and they couldn't travel. After a calm day and they still never came back, we got worried. The next morning, I flew out on our Turbo Beaver on floats to look for them. From a distance, I could see the boat washed up on the shore. We got to Charley's Point and there was the boat up on the rocks and Bernard waving his arms; he was pointing further along and we could see Silas there on the beach and I knew he was dead. It was blowing hard and the water was too rough to land, so we let Bernard know we saw him and then went back to Goose Bay. I knew there was a pond about five miles inside of them and that we could land there and walk out.

I got in touch with the Mounties and told them about what had happened, about our plan, and asked for an escort. There was a young Mountie and he was a bit nervous but I told him it was okay, we could do it, so he came with me. We circled over Bernard a few times and he knew what we were planning to do; then we landed on the pond and walked out to Bernard. It was getting dark by that time. Sure enough, Silas was dead. Bernard hadn't had much to eat for a few days, just some berries, and he was pretty excited by it all but in good shape. Their boat, which had swamped, had come ashore on the rocks that morning and at least he had a tent and some food now.

We made on a good fire and radioed back to Goose Bay what we were doing. There were quite a few bears around so we carried Silas's body back to our fireplace to be safe. We heard there was a **CNR boat** coming up the Bay on its way to Goose Bay and that they would stop and send a small boat in to pick us up. When the fellow from the boat came ashore, it was really rough and it was just a little 10-foot boat; he knew how to handle the boat but we were a bit nervous about getting in with him so we put Silas's body aboard and sent them on, then radioed for another plane to pick us up from the pond. Then we walked back in to the pond and waited to get picked up.

In my work as a forest ranger it was all about firefighting, training people, getting the equipment ready, and fighting fires in the summer. I travelled the coast a lot; visiting sawmills, collecting royalties and stumpage, recording how much lumber they had sawed. I went to Postville, Hopedale, Rigolet, Cartwright, Port Hope Simpson; there were lots of small lumber mills years ago, both private and commercial, right as far as Pinware, Forteau, and Blanc Sablon.

I travelled outside of Labrador a lot for meetings and training. I trained for a month in Arnprior, Ontario, to learn how to train others and then I travelled all over the province and did training in St. John's, Gander, Corner Brook, and Goose Bay. I enjoyed that. When I was getting to the end of my career, we were going to be joining up with the United States for firefighting and that meant travel there a couple times a year. I wasn't interested in that. I retired 1 January 1990.

After retiring, I did some guiding with a local outfitter, including flying with a *National Geographic* crew in to Seal Lake to trace **Mina Hubbard**'s 1905 route. We camped at Seal Lake and used a canoe to explore that portion of the Naskaupi River. It felt awful good to be back in that area again. For all the years I hunted, trapped, and prospected in the Naskaupi and Seal Lake area, I never heard my father or other trappers mention the Hubbard expedition, except for one time my father said that Uncle Bert Blake had gone way in to Ungava with a woman from outside.

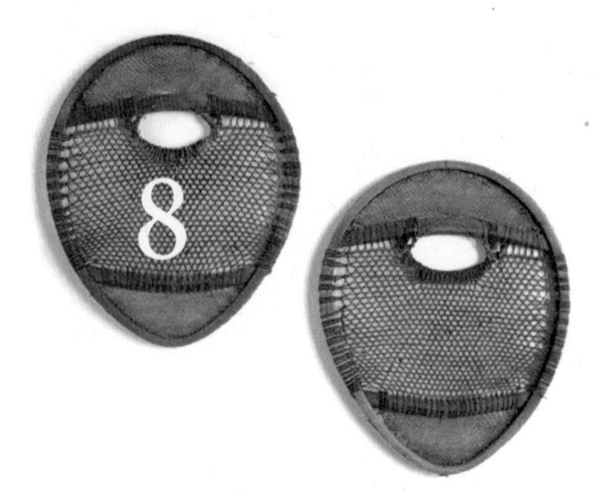


# SALMON FISHING

The salmon fishing in the Kenamu River area, only 12 miles across the Bay from North West River, was a good thing. When the Base started in 1940, there was a good market for fresh salmon. We used to fill up the ice house in Kenemish in the spring; six or seven fishermen shared it. McLeans had a sawmill over there and there was lots of sawdust. We covered the ice with sawdust and it would last all summer. Every third day one motorboat would take the salmon up to the dock in Goose Bay and the armed forces crowd would come down and pick it up in their trucks. There was good money in that, better than trapping, never a failure.

The salmon fishing only lasted for the month of July but our work started a month or so before, getting ready, and lasted a month after, putting stuff away, then all winter knitting and fixing nets in our spare time from trapping and hunting. We made all our own nets; they were always there in the house. I could knit nets when I was almost too small to remember. Mother knit nets in her spare time, so did my father, Russell, and myself too. We had to cut hundreds of pickets for the nets; almost every year a gale of northeast wind would break them off. Some nets had 60 or

70 pickets; we had picket nets, up high in the air so the salmon couldn't jump over them, and on the end of that was a trap net.

When I started commercial salmon fishing with my father in Kenamu, we used to go over there and spend the whole week; we'd always take up the nets on Saturday evening for Sunday. We didn't do nothing on Sunday. I was five or six years old when I started going over there with my father. We used to work really hard at them nets.

My father made enough money at salmon fishing one summer to build us a new house, the one that's still there. Dr. Paddon ordered all the materials for that house and drew up the plan for it, too. Father stayed home that summer and me and Russell did all the fishing. We were really young. I remember one morning when we took the 15-foot **clinker-built** rowboat out and loaded that boat until the salmon were slipping out over the gunnels. Then we'd come ashore, clean them, and leave them in the water all tied together. We'd have a quick cup of tea and go back at it again. There was a steady splash of salmon getting into the net while we were ashore. We went back out and hauled that same net and loaded the boat again.

We had five nets like that. The fish slacked off in the daytime. That was on the upper side of the Kenamu River; then we went to haul the nets on the lower side and there was nothing much there. The winds had everything to do with it. If the winds were up, then the upper side of the river was good and if the winds were down, the lower side was better. I can see the salmon now, jumping around in the boat, and I think a few jumped out. Good fun taking them out of the net but another thing cleaning them all. That was an exceptional catch.

My father only started salmon fishing once the Base came. He started salmon fishing at Otter Creek and Goose River, but that wasn't a very good place. He camped up there and fished for a couple summers but he couldn't get enough salmon there to supply the Base so he moved everything over to the Kenamu River. He realized the Base was a good market, close, and they paid cash, so he wasn't depending on the HBC. There were five or six other people salmon fishing at Kenamu, too.

The first time I saw a vehicle I was with my father; I was seven or eight years old. We took a load of salmon from Kenemish up to the dock in our motorboat. This car came to the dock, with a Major Delaire and Uncle Dan Michelin in it. Uncle Dan worked at the laundry. They came to take the salmon up to the Base and we went with them. Was I ever scared! I didn't know how he'd ever keep the vehicle on that narrow road, going fast like that. I was used to pushing with one foot and steering with my other foot, driving dogs. We went to the mess hall and had a big meal. My father got paid and we bought some apples and oranges at a store and they had ice cream in cones. I didn't know what it was; that was the first time I ever ate ice cream. I was wondering when I'd ever have a chance to get back to Goose Bay for some more. After that when I was in trapping and would get hungry, I could smell all that food they had at the mess hall. Russell told me he was the same.

When we were driving up to the mess hall we went past some machines digging a pipeline for the tank farm, all these bulldozers and backhoes, never saw such a thing before. Uncle Ike Rich told me that when he first saw them, he thought they were horses eating, with big long necks. One time Sid Blake and us took a load of salmon to the Base and Sid pointed to his son Edward working on a crew. I thought he was working awful hard and must be making lots of money.

After Russell and me were old enough to work for wages, Father gave up the salmon fishing.

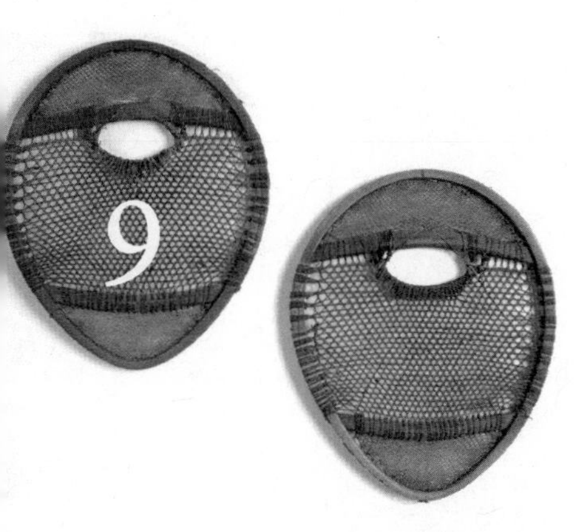

# SEAL HUNTING AND DOGS

The HBC store was the gathering place back in my young days, the place where people met to trade and talk. In the fall of the year, all the big old motorboats were hauled up in front of it. These were 30- and 40-foot wooden motorboats, quite heavy, hauled up by a crowd of men at the end of October for the winter. There might be 20 or 30 men hauling and they used to sing, "To my johnny poker, we will haul this heavy joker, and to my johnny poker, we will 'Hey,'" and everybody would heave on the ropes when we said "hey." It was quite a job. Later on the Grenfell Mission had a little tractor and everybody with a motorboat would hire it and that was the end of hauling by hand. In the spring these boats would all be scraped and painted and the engines gone over, and any repairs made that were needed before they went back in the water.

While all this painting and getting boats ready was being done in April and May, we hunted geese and ducks. The store would be out of basic food by then so the ducks and geese were a welcome sight. There were no freezers to keep food so we ate it fresh and some was bottled. The geese and ducks were really fat, migrating from down south. I've seen a couple times when they still had corn in them, so they got here pretty fast from where they had been feeding. We thought that always made them a good taste; they were always better eating in the spring than the fall, still are. For a long time the spring migratory bird hunt was cut out but when the Innu and Inuit formed their own governments, we gained that back, so now we can get a small number of birds, but still enough.

We'd hunt birds here in Little Lake and out to Sandy Point Run; that was open all winter; that's six or seven miles away. We'd use the dog team to haul the canoes out, tie the dogs on and have food for them, then hunt in canoes. When everywhere else was slow opening up, Sandy Point Run was good.

There was always water open right here by North West River, about a six-mile stretch, open most of the winter. As soon as spring started, it would open quick; we'd usually start hunting around April 25th. We'd usually hunt geese and ducks for about a month or until we had enough. We got our canoes ready, painted them white and put a screen across, called a "fly"; that was usually a piece of plywood to hide behind. You'd have your gun across the gunnels and float amongst the pans of ice, float right up to the ducks and geese. We also wore white clothes, cap and all, so we looked like a piece of ice. The birds were easy to creep up to, but after one shot, they knew. We hunted in the fall, but that was entirely different. In the fall you had to go far, walk over the bogs; we did it, but it was harder.

The same time of year we were hunting birds, we were out on the ice hunting the jar seal. The jar seal was small, maybe 40 to 50 pounds; a couple dogs could eat a jar carcass. We'd hunt between here and 60 or 70 miles out the Bay. After we killed the seals close to North West River, we'd move farther down the Bay.

Around the 20th of April, we'd start hunting jar seals on the **fast ice** with a spear called a ***naulak*** and ***unak***. The *naulak* was a proper arrowhead spear made out of metal with a stick about six or seven feet long with a metal rod on the end of that stick; the arrowhead on the end of the metal rod had a line of about 12 or 14 feet in length which we held in our hand; when the *naulak* went into the seal it turned crosswise and couldn't come out and we were left with the seal on the end of the line; the *unak*, which was the remaining stick with the metal rod in it, was then used to kill the seal if the *naulak* hadn't done so.

The ice on the Bay was about a metre thick. The seals made their holes in the rough ice that had been broke up since it would catch and hold the snow. They only came up on real fine days but with the dog team, you could find every hole; the dogs would get right excited when they smelled the seal hole, tear their feet up and everything going after the seal. If they caught a seal we'd kill it but we wouldn't let them eat it; we never let them eat in the daytime. When Ski-Doos come out, we were lost; we had to wait until we could see the seals on the ice and see where they went down in order to find the hole.

When a mother seal had her young she had about seven holes scattered around. One was the "house" with three or four little holes almost touching each other, and then others scattered about in the area. We usually hunted in groups up to eight or nine people with someone watching each hole but if you didn't have enough people to watch each hole, you put something there to make it look like someone was there. We often used junks of wood so the seal wouldn't come up. Then you'd wait by one hole, standing back to dart the seal when he came up for a breath. A seal could stay under water for about 12 minutes.

The seal would have heard the hunter and dogs come to the hole and know there was danger and would swim around and check out other breathing holes in order to safely surface. We could tell if a seal was coming to a hole because as he circled around it, the water would start to swirl and come up through the hole; when we saw that, we went on alert, held our spear up, and got ready to dart when we saw his whiskers. The seals were very fast and could sometimes come up and flip over and be gone before you had a chance to dart them.

One time, Uncle Piercy and Uncle Olin put their mitts, coats, everything by the holes. Uncle Piercy put his cap over one hole. Uncle Olin went to another hole to wait to dart, and all at once he saw Uncle Piercy with his head stuck up out of the hole and he thought he must of fell in, so he went running over to help and saw it was a little seal had come up the hole and had Uncle Piercy's cap on his head. The seal had no ears to hold the cap up so it was right down over his eyes and he couldn't see nothing; there were lots of stories like that from out on the Bay.

I remember the first seal I ever darted was when my father took me down around Mulligan. In the evening we went ashore to Mulligan and I was anxious to show everybody my seal. Uncle Dan Campbell was standing there and I told him that I had darted my first seal that day. He said jokingly, "that was some foolish old seal to let you dart him." I was about 10 or 11 years old. I had been trying for seals before that, without any luck.

Jar seals were for dog food, and we ate them, too. We sold the pelts of young jar seals to the HBC and boots, mitts, and jackets were made from the adult seals. Their skins were small and not very thick, not like a harp seal. Some harp sealskins were used for boots after they were well cleaned. We used sealskin to make **traces** and lash lines for lashing our stuff on the komatik. It would last for evermore unless the dogs ate it. Ruth's mother made me a pair of sealskin mitts one time to go caribou hunting in the Mealies and a dog ate my mitts.

In later years, jar seals were a good price. Some years we had longer to hunt than others, depending on the weather and ice conditions. Some years we didn't get many; some years we got a lot. I remember one spring I had a lot and they were worth about $60 each at the HBC. I cleaned some and Aunt Edna Campbell cleaned a lot for me, and so did Mrs. [Ellen] Oliver, while I kept on hunting.

Most of the seals were darted right down through the head as they come up the hole; they came up and we darted down; they were killed instantly, a good way to kill them, a lot better than guns. With guns you lose a lot but you don't lose any with a spear. They were quite heavy to haul up; sometimes they would hold onto the bottom of the ice with their claws; I used to have my hands right bleeding at times. Sometimes you'd get an old one, about 150 pounds; they were some heavy. Sometimes he'd go right slack on the line, just like a fish. Then you'd walk back from the hole as far as you could go; if he wasn't hit in the head, if he made a motion to go, he'd drag you right to the edge of the hole and you scrabbling to dig your heels in, always ready to let go. Sometimes you'd get the mother and baby seal both; they come up together and you put the dart through one and into the other.

When you're darting seals, you gotta stay still, can't move your feet, just turn your head. Sometimes when we were hunting them with guns, we'd crawl after them on our bellies and act like a seal; you'd stick your legs up and flick them like a flipper, scratch the ice, act like another seal. They'd watch you and when they looked down, you'd crawl towards them right fast. Uncle Stewart used to put white tape on his face like whiskers, some funny looking. We had a ***taloouk***; we made them to hold in front of us when we were walking up to the seals; it was a square frame of wood, covered with white cloth, with a handle on it and a bar across the middle and another stick to pull up on, that would tighten the cloth and you'd keep down behind that and keep moving closer when the seal looked away, stop when he looked at you. The morning was no good for this because it would be noisy walking on the crusty snow, but when the snow got soft, it worked good.

We made sealskin boots for our dogs for when we went seal hunting. The dogs would get so excited after the seals, they'd tear up their feet on the crust in the spring, didn't even need to be chasing a seal, just from running. We'd cut out a square of sealskin, put some holes through for their front toenails and tie them on with line that wouldn't shrink. You had to be careful not to make them too tight and check them during the day. Sometimes running along, their boots would come off and you'd pick them up and put them back on the dogs when you stopped the next time. Sometimes when we stopped, we had an armful of dog boots.

We used Stockholm tar on their feet. Dogs used to love that tar; they'd see you coming in the morning with the bucket of tar and they'd fall over on their backs with their feet stuck up; they knew it was gonna feel good. Sometimes you'd use tar and boots and sometimes just tar. One old feller tarred his own feet after he tarred his dogs' feet. Our feet were wet all the time in the spring in our sealskin boots, and sweating, then they'd dry up and crack. We'd put tar on our sealskin boots if they got thin and they'd be waterproof again for a while.

In the spring as soon as the ice started breaking up, the harp seals would come up the Bay; that's the same ones they kill off the coast of Newfoundland and Labrador. Around the 24th of May or first of June, we'd put out our nets for the harp seals. We'd set them in about five or six **fathoms** of water at the inside end and twenty or more fathom at the outer end. We'd set the nets out around the mouth of North West River or out in Sandy Point Run or down around Green Island. The harp seals come up the Bay chasing the **capelin**; that's all I ever saw them eat. Their bellies would be right full of capelin. Sometimes you'd get a dozen seals in one net. Working at seal nets went on for about three weeks. It was a lot of work and we used to work hard, from daylight to after dark.

We'd sink our nets quite deep so the ice wouldn't take them. Sometimes the ice would come in over them and we wouldn't see them for a week until the wind changed and blew the ice away. The harp seal nets were about 16- or 17-inch mesh, stretched mesh. We'd make our own nets in the winter, in the house. I made all my own nets, trout, salmon, and seal. A seal net would be about 125 to 150 feet long, two joined to make that length; they were called a "fleet" because there were two joined together. They were made in half lengths because they would have been too heavy to handle if they were all in one. When you put them out, you joined the two together.

The seal nets were set in a straight line. We'd put an anchor with a couple hundred feet of rope on the inside end, then run the net out with a good big anchor and the same length of rope on the outside end. The anchor would be 25 or 30 pounds. On the inside end, we had a prior pole to mark our net; it was a long thin stick about 12- to 14-feet long, as long as we could get. On that we had a piece of rope tied to the foot rope of the seal net with a good big rock tied on. The prior pole would stick up above the water five or six feet and the ice could go over it but wouldn't hook into the net. We tied rocks as sinkers all along the foot rope, about three or four pounds each, about 14 or 16 rocks on the whole fleet of net. The net would sink to the bottom; you couldn't even see it under the water; all you could see was the prior pole above water. Very seldom did anyone lose their net to the ice. We had corks along the head rope, made them ourselves, cut them out of a big piece of cork.

Everybody had their nets set in the same area and you'd see all these prior poles sticking up. When the seals hit the nets, they died fast if they'd been underwater for a while catching fish and had no breath left. We caught them when they were feeding on capelin. Sometimes when we went to check our nets, we couldn't even see the prior poles; we had to wait for the tide to slacken so the poles would stick up. After about three weeks, the harp seal fishery was over.

Green Island was the hot spot for seal nets; that's three or four miles from North West River; any place where the seals came close to shore in deep water was good but the deeper the water, the harder to haul the net. We went out to haul our nets in our motorboat and towed our rowboat behind. We'd tie the motorboat to the prior pole and then use the rowboat to haul the net. When we got a load in the rowboat then we'd load them from there into the motorboat. Two men in a boat could barely get a harp over the side of the rowboat. When it was loaded down to the gunnels with seals and the motorboat being so high, we had to get them up into the motorboat. For that we used a **parbuckle**, sort of like a **come-along**: we tied a couple lines onto the rising of the motorboat, put the rope around the seal, and rolled them up on the line. Then, when you got home in the big motorboat, you had to offload them again into the rowboat and from there, you'd get them up on the gunnel and roll them out right into the shallow water by the beach.

I started going to seal nets with my father when I was seven or eight. I couldn't handle the seals but I wanted to go with him. We'd go ashore on Green Island and boil the kettle and wait for the tide to fall back, a whole crowd of fellas. We'd have guns and we'd be shooting at marks with our .22s or steaming up to **bottle-nosed divers** and shooting at them. I loved that stuff, wouldn't miss it; of course, I could only go on the weekend. If I was in school, I'd be some excited to get home and ask my father how many seals he got.

Everybody in town with a dog team was working at seals at the same time. The whole beachfront along town was strung with seals, rotten and stinking in the summer. We used to keep the carcasses in the water if we weren't ready to skin them yet. We skinned them quick because it was getting warm weather; we cleaned the hides, and nailed them on the house to dry. I remember our old house right covered with big old harp sealskins and more waiting to go on. Sometimes we got old jars in the harp seal nets. The old jar in the spring is no good; we called them double hair, the old hair coming out and the new hair starting to grow, and the skins were no good but we still salted the meat for dog food. There was no sale for skins in my young days, not until after I was married.

Most people had dog teams; my father always had a dog team and so did I when I got older. In June, we put away our seals for dog food. We'd salt that meat and blubber for the dogs for use the next winter, 'cause we didn't get seals in the fall. There were seals in Lake Melville in the fall, but we were busy getting ready for trapping so we didn't bother with them in the fall.

We skinned the seal, cut it up, put it in layers in wooden barrels; in some barrels, there'd be a layer of meat then a layer of salt, and so on, until the barrel was full. In others, there was layers of meat alternated with layers of fat. That meat stored with fat kept well because the fat turned to oil and preserved it. The third way of keeping seal meat was barrels containing layers of fat and salt. That seal fat was some stinking. Then we put heads on the barrels with a rock on top so the lid wouldn't blow off or the dogs get into it.

The barrels were kept in front of the house above the high-water mark. Seals were all skinned down the bank in front of the houses on the landwash; big old seals, between 200 and 300 pounds each. Everything came in barrels them days, pork and beef and molasses, so we had lots of barrels for storage. My father and mother both worked at skinning and cleaning seals, as did me and Russell. We cleaned out some of the seal **puddicks**; they were right full of capelin and we put that on the gardens for fertilizer; we used seal guts for garden fertilizer, too.

For my team of seven huskies, I needed about 25 or 30 old harps to salt down and carry them through the next winter. We'd start feeding them on salted seal meat in November. You didn't feed it to them salt; you cut a hole in the ice, poked holes in the meat and tied pieces on a line and soaked it for about a week before it was ready for the dogs to eat. Sometimes we put it in brin bags to soak; there was always lots of brin bags them days from supplies at the HBC. We fed the raw seal meat to the dogs after soaking it. If we went away for a long period, we couldn't carry enough seal meat and blubber to feed them; it would have been too heavy. We would buy corn meal from the store, made purpose for dogs, and cook that for them. We'd put pieces of seal fat or meat in with the corn meal; they loved that and they'd work good on it. When they were eating lots of seal, they were really healthy; their fur would get right shiny and healthy-looking. They had to have the fat if they were working; the huskies needed a lot of grease.

When we had fresh seal in the spring, we fed the dogs the meat fresh. When we were hunting out on the ice, we'd feed them fresh seal every night. We used to eat a lot of seal meat back then, too, but I don't eat much now. We were working hard them days, always hungry; we'd eat anything you threw at us. You could cook it any way; the liver was exceptionally good, old harp liver. I'd like some right now. We used to bottle the meat, too. Bottled seal meat is really good.

To make a seal net, you'd carve out a wooden knitting needle. To make a 16-inch mesh, you'd make an eight-inch card of wood. You'd buy the twine from the HBC; it was all cotton and would only last a couple years. All winter long you'd be mending and knitting nets, right in the kitchen. You'd work at that in bad weather. Father never stopped at it. I used to get some sick of it. Seal net didn't take too long because it was such big mesh. You bought a big piece of cork and sawed out floats with a hand saw and smoothed them and put a crack in them for on the head rope. The head ropes were right and left, twisted different ways so they wouldn't kink. One was rolled right and one rolled left with the corks in between. You needed a lot of rocks to tie on the foot rope.

The seals don't come in the Bay any more like they used to; they used to be plentiful in the springtime; you could almost walk across the Bay on their heads. Now when you go down around the grassy islands in the spring, you only see the odd one. I blame it on too many boats chasing them, people shooting at them. In my day, we didn't dare shoot at seals. The old people told us that the shooting drove them away. You wouldn't dare let an old person catch you shooting at a seal. Now it seems like there are more harp seals around this end of the Bay in the fall. Many get caught in the Bay at freeze-up time.

We ate seals, fed them to the dogs, used their skins for clothing and sleds, dog harnesses, traces, and boots, and many other things; they were really important to our way of life. I used to sell a lot of seal meat to the stores in Goose Bay; people from the Coast and from Newfoundland working on the Base were right excited to get seal meat in the spring; we'd get 15 cents a pound — good money in it. We used to have whales come up here, minkes and belugas, and swordfish, too, but they were pretty rare.

Some trappers would use the biggest old harp sealskin caught in the spring for a sled on the trapline. First in the fall, you'd use it with the flesh side out and after dragging it around for a while, any flesh or grease left on it would be cleaned off, and it would be right soft and perfectly clean. Once it was cleaned, you used it with the hair side out and your stuff inside on the flesh side. It slipped along right good on the hair side, as long as you had it sliding with the grain of the hair. Some trappers took one husky dog with them and they'd haul that sealskin loaded with all their stuff. I could go off for a week on my cross-country path with just a sealskin full of my supplies. Once the dog got used to hauling it, not the first year in the country but the second year, that old dog knew, and if he came to a **deadfall** where he might hook in with the sealskin, he'd go around it, rather than try going over it. They'd get used to that. You'd have a harness on the dog and a trace going back to the sealskin. You folded the nose of the sealskin in to make a point, and tied the trace to that, and then tied it close to the dog so it would follow him through the trees, maybe three or four feet behind him. The trapper would walk ahead on his snowshoes making a path, because dogs were no good in deep snow, and on traplines in heavy wooded country the snow never drift and got hard. When the old dog would come out on a river or lake where the snow was drifted hard, he'd be some glad to run around easy.

When I was going to school in St. John's, I ran into Tom Edmunds and Bill Manak from Makkovik. They told me that they walked up this way cross-country from Makkovik one time, hauling their sleds and hunting. They came to a place and saw what they thought was a wolf but then they saw that he was dragging something and figured out it was a dog. Pretty soon, they saw a man coming on snowshoes and it turned out to be Uncle Byron Chaulk in on his trapline from Mulligan with his dog hauling his sealskin sled. They stayed with him a couple days while he made the rounds of his traps and then went back to Mulligan with him. They said they stayed in Mulligan for a few days and people were awful kind to them. Uncle Byron brought them up to North West River with his dog team for supplies, then took them down to Valley's Bight to start on the portage back to Makkovik. They couldn't get over how good his sealskin sled slipped along with a big load and told everybody in Makkovik and Postville about it. They said that within a couple years, everybody up that way was using sealskin sleds on their traplines.

My father told me a story about Reverend Burry. Reverend Burry liked to hunt and he had a big team, too, so he needed lots of seals for dog feed. Out on the ice where the pressure cracks crossed the Bay, a few miles apart, there were these pressure ridges and the seals used to come up through those cracks. Those were the old male seals and the hunters could never get them. Reverend Burry told all the men that they'd go out in the morning and he had a plan to get them seals. He arranged for the Mulligan people to come up and meet our people from here. He said there were 400 or 500 seals all along those cracks, and they would drive their dogs up close to them and let the seals dive back down. Then everybody would run all along the crack, 30 or 40 men, and wait for the seals to come back up and breathe, and then spear them. So they tried it, ran up to them and spread out along the crack and never saw another seal. You could never get the old ones.

Husky dogs seem to know if their driver is lost and will return to the last place they camped. I remember one time when me and John Edmunds were seal hunting on Lake Melville; we had camped on the end of Dry Island and then went on the next day, headed down the middle of the Bay for Lowlands. A blizzard came on, snow and wind, and we weren't sure of our directions; I tried to make my leader dog turn towards land but he wouldn't turn even though I tried and tried; he wouldn't listen; he wanted to go his own way so I finally let him go 'cause I didn't know where we were. He took us straight back to where we had left camp that morning. I had been trying to drive him the wrong way at first but then I let him follow his own way. That happened a number of times and I learned to trust my leader; dogs have a wonderful sense of direction; they know.

I loved my dogs, still dream about them; they were really a good team. The breed of the dog is important. I had two Siberian huskies, smartest dogs I ever seen. One was my leader; I could talk to him and he understood. The others were Labrador huskies. What made a good team was lots of seal meat and lots of use. First using them in the fall after lying about all summer, they were no good; let them run about for a couple days and then they were good for it. I used to go 80 miles in one day, over to Beaver Brook at the foot of the Mealies. I'd haul six or seven caribou back. In the spring, in March, when the snow was froze on top and good going, I could go over there in one day. One time, I remember, I came in down here at the Portage Path with my seven huskies, hauling five caribou on the komatik. I had left Beaver Brook that morning. Sandy Riche and a couple other fellas were there; they could hardly believe I came that far in one day. Sandy said, "Look, them dogs aren't even tired, they didn't even lie down."

You couldn't do nothing without dogs. I hauled my own wood and wood for others with my dogs. I didn't loan my team because your dogs wouldn't listen to another person. People that didn't have dogs either hired another team or hired another man to do the work. If my dogs were sick, I'd borrow a couple dogs to make up a team to go caribou hunting. My dogs were local. If I knew somebody that had good dogs, I'd ask them to save me some puppies. Murdock Broomfield had Siberian huskies and I asked him to save me a brood and he gave me three — gave them to me, didn't sell them.

I built a pen for the puppies and reared them up. When they got older, they'd sometimes get sick and die. I tried to maintain seven dogs. They were best when they were around three years old; when they got about nine years old, you couldn't use them in a team of young dogs. Some could go on to age 12. The old dogs were used on the trapline, a single dog to haul a sled or your sealskin; they were good for that. On the Coast, they needed bigger teams, maybe 10 or 12 dogs because they travelled longer distances than we ever did, took their whole families and hauled big loads. On the Coast, they had access to seals for dog food all year-round. Here, we only got seals in the spring.

It was a lot of work having dogs, feeding them even when they weren't in use. In my father's time they used to put [keep] dogs down on John Bull Island, down off Butter and Snow. On John Bull Island in the spring, they were close to the seal nets so we'd throw a seal or two to them when we were coming back from our nets. I only remember that once in my time, having them on John Bull.

When my father was commercial salmon fishing over at Kenamu, we had our dogs with us. They ate the salmon heads and the gills; we never had to feed them anything else over there. In the spring when I was trapping, I'd use the dogs to go up and strike up my traps. I'd be gone less than two weeks. I'd take food for them. Husky dogs can go five or six days with no food if they're fat. Only once do I remember me and my father taking them into the country with us; we were going to be gone six days across country and the dogs just walked along with us; one dog hauled the sealskin; we took cornmeal and seal fat, enough for two or three nights.

I used to roam around a lot. When you had dogs, you could go anywhere. Them were the good old days; it was some hard work but I was strong and healthy. I'd travel around, put up a tent at night; it was a wonderful free life. Our family never travelled by dog team except to come down from Red Wine River in the spring. Grandfather never had a dog team that I remember.

I was young when I took over care of the dogs; I guess I was about seven. I learned to make the harness and traces, put tassels on them, made them real fancy. I'd hook one dog up to a komatik and we'd ride around; that was our real play. We'd ride around town or up in the lake. In the morning when you harnessed them up, you'd put your leg over the dog's back to hold them there. I was little and I had two dogs that were so tall, they would take off with me on their backs like a horse. They were strong; you couldn't hold them back if they were after something. In later years, I used to take Kathy [daughter of Irene] and Irving out riding around when they were small, give them a ride up around the lake; could those dogs ever go; they were anxious to get off the chain and run.

In about 1962, I only had two dogs left and I gave them up for snowmobiles. I'd been watching the snowmobiles for about four years. They were all passing me. I remember wanting to go seal hunting and I went down to the HBC and talked to the manager, Mr. Jeffries, and I told him I'd like to buy a snowmobile but I didn't have any money. He told me to take one and go on and pay for it when I got the money. I went out hunting and made enough that spring to pay for it and more; it cost 750 dollars, a 6-horsepower Bombardier, the best machine to haul that I ever had. I worked some hard that year, just kept going. I never stopped.

One time in the HBC, I heard Richard Oliver say he got a komatik stuck in the slush with a load of wood on it. Whoever was there offered him their team to help out and he said that he had to wait until it froze. He said the way that it was stuck, seven devils hauling side by side would never get it out. I could just picture it in my mind. When I was young and we heard about somebody doing something bad or in trouble, there was always seven devils around, chasing them or whatever.

They always talked about the mailman who ran the mail between here and Rigolet (see Ritch, 1977); he was a hard old man. They were never supposed to work on Sunday them days but he left Rigolet on a Sunday with his load of mail and he was coming up across the Bay, going along good, when all of a sudden his dogs went wild, right frightened; he had his whip dragging behind the komatik like they always did and once in a while he'd feel something pluck at his whip. He looked behind and there was seven devils after him and they'd run ahead and smack their hoofs on the back of the komatik, broke it up and everything. He went in to Sebaskashu and when they got there the dogs were so frightened, they went right in the house, right through the window, komatik and all. I never heard what happened to the devils that were chasing him. Later when he was hunting around Ambrose Island, he went out hunting on Sunday and saw a devil sitting up on a rock out in the water, so he fired at him and the devil went ass over kettle into the water and was never seen since. That's some of the stories I heard when I was young.

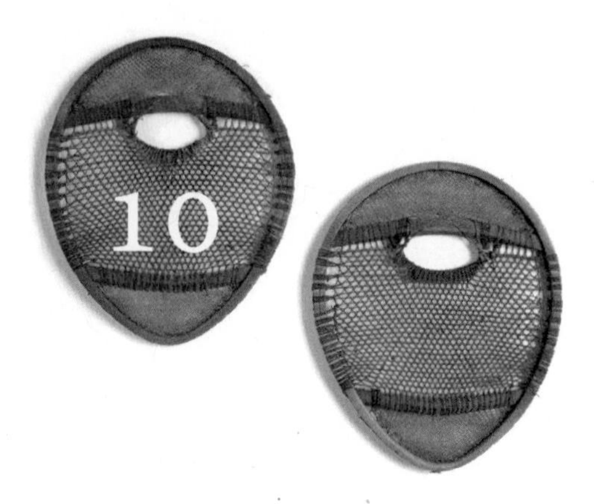


# CARIBOU HUNTING IN THE MEALIES

Caribou hunting usually started in January, right after New Year's. We'd been home from the trapline for Christmas and New Year's and started thinking about fresh meat. The Bay was usually froze up by the 10th of January, sometimes earlier. We'd leave from here on dog team and head for the Mealies. We'd cross the Bay over to Adams Point, which is about 14 miles, then we'd head on down along the shore to a place we thought might be good to hunt from. We'd set up camp at the foot of the mountains and then climb the mountains on snowshoes. We'd hunt on top of the Mealies, hunt every day until we got our caribou; sometimes we'd get them the first day; sometimes we'd have to hunt a week or more; sometimes we got nothing, but we usually got our caribou.

It was the Mealy Mountain caribou herd that we hunted. They were a lot bigger animals than the caribou we hunt now from the George River herd. That Mealy Mountain herd wasn't migratory; they walked around a little and calved all around the Coast. There was a lot of bog and they calved in that mostly. Even if we got none, that didn't mean there wasn't any Mealy Mountain caribou; it just meant they were on the other side of the Mealies. We didn't know where they were. Years later, after I worked with Wildlife and was flying around in helicopter, I saw them over on the other side of the Mealies, over near the Gulf of St. Lawrence shore, and people were hunting them over there. But that was too far for us to go and we had no way of knowing where they were them days.

Along the Mealies, there's about seven places where I've hunted, seven places to get in over the mountains; you can't just go anywhere; some places were brooks, some places were **leads**. You'd pick either place you wanted to try. Beaver Brook was the furthest place we would go to although I have been much further than that. Beaver Brook was the best caribou hunting place and the easiest route to get in to the top of the mountains. Beaver Brook is about 70 miles from North West River. That was our main place. I've hunted Shellbird Island, Peter Lucy's Brook, Shoal River, the Birches, Mink Brook, and Between the Rivers — that's between Big River and Little River. You could climb up the mountains at any of those places, walk in easy on snowshoes. Once we got on top, we could see all over and go most anywhere to hunt caribou. Sometimes we got them right on the edge of the mountain and sometimes we had to walk a long ways in, and a few times we had to take camping gear, dogs, komatik, the whole works, way in over the mountains until we got to what we called "the green woods" and set up our camp there. I don't know how far that would be but it was a full day's walk, so maybe 15 or 20 miles.

When we went for our day hunts, we left the dogs out at our camp and spent all day hunting on the mountains. We'd usually leave an hour before daylight to go up the mountain. If we killed our caribou, then the next day we'd bring the dogs in but no komatik. We'd tie their traces around our waists and they'd help us walk up the mountain; five or six dogs' traces tied around your waist, and you just hoping they wouldn't see a caribou or you'd be gone, good-bye Joe. That never happened often, but sometimes we'd run into caribou on the way back in with the dogs.

We'd tie two caribou together and have the dogs haul them what we call "on the dead"; that meant with no sled, just two caribou hooked together, and the dogs would haul them out to our camp at the foot of the mountain. We'd do that until we got all our caribou out; bring two out every day. We'd **paunch** them as soon as we killed them and leave them whole, not skinned or butchered.

Caribou hunting took an average of two weeks with a dog team; we'd prepare for two weeks, food for us and the dogs. Sometimes we'd be gone seven days or as long as three weeks. Some years there were none, but I can only remember two years when there was no caribou at all.

The first time I went, I was 14. I went with my father. We'd been trapping for the fall and came home for Christmas and New Year's. After New Year's, we went over to the Mealies with Juddy Blake and Norman Budgell, who also had dog teams. We went as far as Shellbird Island, not as far as Beaver Brook. The caribou were right out there close. In the tent that first night, Juddy told me that if we got up to some caribou, I could have the first shot. I didn't believe him but in the morning, we weren't long running into some caribou, six in a company, and Juddy handed over the gun and I shot my first caribou. Juddy told me I could get married now that I had shot my first caribou.

That was a good trip but we had an awful batch of snow while we were gone and had a hard time coming back. We had to walk all the way home in front of the dogs, packing a snowshoe track for them so they could haul the heavy load. Often you could only bring part of your load at one time and then go back later for the rest. From here to Beaver Brook in the winter, it would take two days. We'd camp along the shore as soon as it was getting dark. At the end of February or in March when the snow was getting settled down and hard and good going, and longer days, you made better time. I've gone from here to Beaver Brook in one day.

It was a busy time 'cause you had to cook for your dogs. We took corn meal and seal fat for the dogs and a bit of meat once in a while but we never fed them caribou meat. Husky dogs can go three or four days with no food and it doesn't make any difference to them; they can still work hard. While hunting caribou, we might kill a chance porcupine or snare a few rabbits. There were always lots of white partridges but we wouldn't shoot at them because we didn't want to frighten the caribou. Once we had caribou, we didn't need partridges; we always had lots at home. Sometimes going along, we'd stop at Shoal River and fish for sea trout and catch lots for us and the dogs, some of them four and five pounds. It's all fished out now, nothing like that left. Only people with dog teams could get over there to fish them days.

We went over there hunting every year; sometimes I went with others, sometimes by myself. You had to be awful careful up there on the Mealies, 2,400 to 2,500 feet elevation with no trees; it could get rough and storms could come up awful quick. It was awful cold. Some days we would get to the top of the Mealies and have to come back, it was too cold. You'd take your mitt off to pull the trigger and your finger would freeze. We had mitts on strings so we didn't lose them when we flicked them off to shoot; they'd blow away, not a tree in sight for them to tangle up in. We'd get lots of frostbite, neck and face all peeling; you'd freeze and wouldn't even know it. We always had a shawl over our heads, just peeking out under our caps.

I think that first time was the only time I ever went caribou hunting with my father. Other years I'd go with Henry Blake, Uncle Stewart Michelin, Harold Blake, lots of fellas. I almost lived over there in the wintertime. Our family would usually use eight or nine caribou a year. We might get them all one time or might make a couple trips. Sometimes with a team of seven dogs, you could bring back four or five caribou. I remember one time in the spring when it was good going, I brought back six; that's all I could fit on the komatik. After we had a caribou hunt, we'd head back up the Naskaupi to our traps around the 15th of February. By February you could start to feel the sun in the middle of the day. We fitted it all in somehow.

It was all snowshoe-walking on the Mealies, good on top where the snow was packed hard. Climbing up was hard until you got a track made. We usually hunted in pairs, usually three or four pairs of us. Everybody would go in to the mountain together and stop on top and boil the kettle 'cause there was no wood inside. It would take about two hours to go up the mountain. After we boiled the kettle, then each pair would strike off in a different direction. It was long days; we wouldn't turn back until dark, get back to our camp after ten at night; a couple times I spent the night in there in a **barricade**. It was too stormy to come on in the dark. There were no trees for protection and very little wood for fuel.

Myself, Clayton, Bill, Brian all hunted together, also Charley Ikey, and Johnny Edmunds. Johnny was deaf, couldn't hear nothing. He was a good worker, good hunter, an awful fine man. I learned a lot from him. He had no dogs so he'd go with me. Bill and Clayton used their fathers' teams. They each had big teams. I went with Uncle Stewart a couple times. He had a big team. Harold Blake had his father, Pleamon's [Philemon Blake's] team, then his own team on the end of it.

What a change once we had snowmobiles; you could go over to the Mealies, get your caribou and be back the same day, an awful difference. We had to make a snowshoe path first, and then 15 or 20 minutes up the mountain on snowmobile. The snowmobiles had lights so you could come back at night. There's only two places I used for going up on snowmobile; one was Between the Rivers and one was Mink Brook. Each of those places had a little fall; if you could get a straight run you could get up and over. You needed a couple feet of snow to get in there. Once you got to the top on snowmobile, you could run around anywhere. It was fun.

One time I went hunting with Uncle Stewart on his big old red Autoboggan. Him and Sid Blake had one each. Uncle Stewart bought his from Silas Baikie; they weren't around very long. They were powerful machines but they gave their share of trouble, too much maintenance. They had a track with big old metal cleats; they were really noisy. Me and Uncle Stewart went to Little River and camped there; there was already a big crowd there, nine or 10 tents. We saw a plane fly over and then it come back and landed and it was Hank Shouse and his son, Jimmy; Jimmy was just a little boy then. Hank and Jimmy came in our tent for a lunch. I remember Uncle Stewart put a cloth down on the brush in front of Jimmy for him to eat on, and told him that was an Innu tablecloth. We got talking and of course we asked him if he saw any caribou. We knew the caribou were around because we had talked to people who had been hunting. Hank said he wasn't supposed to tell us [by law, pilots weren't supposed to tell where they saw herds], but if it was him, he'd go hunting at Big Point.

Well, Uncle Stewart packed up some quick, doing 10 jobs at one time, getting ready to leave. We got to Mink Brook, about a couple hours further on, and there was a bunch of caribou walking way out on the ice, like they were crossing the Bay. Uncle Stewart told me to stop the machine and he got off and went on with his gun. He started shooting at them, long shots, and I saw the caribou dropping. They started running and Uncle Stewart started running after them. He had his gun held over his head, crosswise, and his hands spread out to make it look like antlers. He looked just like a caribou, when he was end-on. He shot all ours right there on the ice, then we went on to Big Point and camped there; there was a big crowd there. They all heard the news from Hank.

Coming back across the Bay on the Auto-boggan, the throttle or something gave out; it would go, but awful slow. We didn't know anything about snowmobiles. Uncle Stewart was behind and I was driving; the motor was on the back of the Auto-boggan. Uncle Stewart found where to lift up on the throttle and it would take right off so he held that up all the way home. On the way, he tapped me on the shoulder and said he never thought he'd be crossing the Bay on a big old **emmett**.

When we got home, we got bogged down on the bank by Uncle Stewart's house. We had to go up the bank and the machine dug in. He got off to push; he put his shoulder against the back of it and grabbed hold underneath and I guess he got his finger in a sprocket or something, and cut his finger off. I didn't know what had happened; I couldn't see him; I saw some blood on the snow and the next thing I saw, he was running towards the hospital. When he got by Leslie's house, next door, he looked back and said "C'mon boy." I think it was his little finger.

Another time I was down caribou hunting with Uncle Stewart and our tow bar on the komatik was bent awful bad. It was curled around and we never tried to straighten it because we didn't think we could bend the metal. We met Edward Blake and Jack Budgell on Sid's machine; they were going down and we were coming back. Uncle Stewart was telling them and showing them his tow bar and Jack walked over to it and grabbed it in his hands and straightened it out, buckled it across his knee, same as nothing. Uncle Stewart laughed some hard. I think we were gone about five nights that trip.

A lot of Innu were camped at Little River that trip, a bunch of men from Sheshatshiu. They had killed a lot of caribou before that and had covered them in snow; they had walked to the Mealies and hauled their sleds. They would skin the caribou and cut the legs off, then wrap it all up in the skin and tie that with a line and haul it back. They knew how to do it.

One year I went over caribou hunting on the 10th or 12th of December; I went with Brian Michelin and Bernard Chaulk. We went down to Green Island and struck across the Bay in order to avoid Sandy Point Run, which was always open, even in the winter. We went out to the big shoal and then straight across to Adams Point. The ice was barely strong enough. There was no snow until we got almost to the shoreline on the other side; there was snow over there. Bernard had a team and I had a team and Brian was with me; we used Brian's dog with mine. A couple days after we got there, Russell Groves and Juddy Blake came and they told us that the ice we had crossed on was all gone when they tried to cross. They had to go back and cross at a different place. We got nine caribou down to Beaver Brook. I guess we didn't go trapping that fall since we were caribou hunting in December. We were sure glad to have the caribou meat that year.

The caribou were fat at that time of the year. The fattest time for the does over there was in December. I think it's different with the George River herd; the does are fatter at different times, plus they do a lot more travelling. We used to be crazy about eating the fat from the Mealy Mountain caribou but now we can hardly eat the fat from the George River caribou, totally different taste, not good like fat from the Mealy Mountain herd. They have different feed and aren't migratory. The old people really noticed the difference. The George River caribou would be about two-thirds the size of the Mealy Mountain caribou.

Another year we went over in the Mealies hunting caribou just before Christmas. We camped at Adams Point on our way over. Bernard's dogs gave out, way too fat, and not used to running; mine were pretty fat, too. We didn't feed them for a few nights and then they were good for it. We

Louie Montague playing the fiddle at Green Point on Grand Lake, 1970s. Photo: Elmer Lakata.

Prospecting: Uncle Austin Montague and Louie Montague, 1957, Moran Lake area. Prospectors brought rock specimens back to camp and broke them up in the evenings to look for ores like copper, lead, and zinc; headphones were attached to Geiger counters to check rock for uranium; they wore Geiger counters all day while prospecting. Photo: Don Huxter.

Louie at his cabin on the Naskaupi River, using a hand plane on a fur-stretching board, September 2, 2012. Other fur-stretching boards are to his left. Photo: Elizabeth Dawson.

Louie in front of his cabin, looking southeast down the Naskaupi River, September 2, 2012. Photo: Elizabeth Dawson.

View from Louie's cabin looking south into the Red Wine River; Mount Elizabeth in background.
September 2, 2012. Photo: Elizabeth Dawson.

Louie making shavings with a crooked knife he made himself, September 2012. Photo: Elizabeth Dawson.

Louie with bear trap, Naskaupi River, 2003. Photo: Louie Montague.

Ulu made by Louie from hand saw blade with caribou antler handle and stand. January 2012. Photo: Elizabeth Dawson.

Louie at his tilt on the Naskaupi River, built in 1968; the tin roof was added to protect tilt from black bears. September 2, 2012. Photo: Elizabeth Dawson.

Looking south towards the mouth of the Naskaupi River where it empties into Grand Lake. Cape Law in the distance; mouth of Crooked River on left. September 1, 2012. Photo: Elizabeth Dawson.

Looking to the north from Hegrew Lake at the foot of the once powerful Hegrew Rapids, showing willow- and poplar-covered islands that have formed with reduced outflow of Naskaupi River; Mount Sawyer on left. September 2, 2012. Photo: Elizabeth Dawson.

Spring goose hunt at the Rapids. April 2011. Photo: Elizabeth Dawson.

Liz and Louie, Easter 2012, at Elizabeth Dawson's Tickle Island cabin. Self photo.

Freshly cooked flummies beside the tent stove; plucked partridges in background waiting to be cooked. April 2011. Photo: Elizabeth Dawson.

Klim and other supplies in Labrador Heritage Society's Hudson's Bay Company Museum, North West River, May 2011. Photo: Elizabeth Dawson.

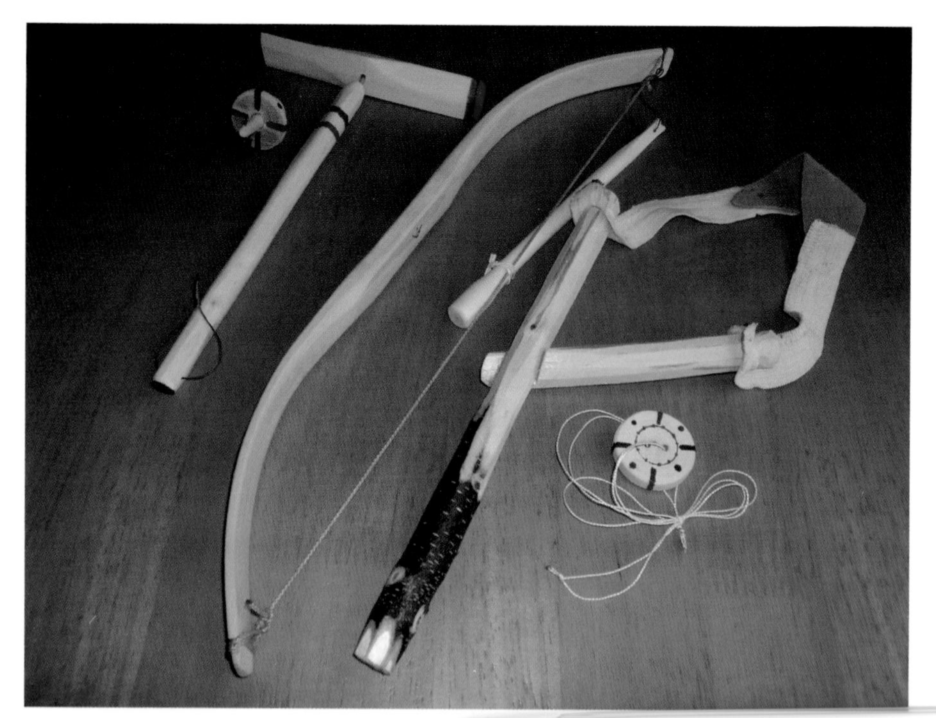

Louie continues to make toys similar to those he received as a child. Upper left to lower right: spin top (made from wooden thread spool); windmill; bow and arrow; slingshot; spinner (sometimes a large button was used instead of a wooden disc). Photo: Elizabeth Dawson.

Wood and fabric craft made by Louie and Ruth Montague, 1990s. Photo: Louie Montague.

were camped at Little River, about 200 feet or so from the shore, at the edge of the woods. The caribou were on the marshes, lots of them, so we didn't have to go in on the mountains that time. We got our caribou and were hauling them off the marshes when a storm came on.

There was quite a bit of snow when we went over but there came a southeast gale of wind down off the mountains and it took the snow out just like somebody shovelled it away, wind and rain like you wouldn't believe. The ice all blowed off the shore [away from shore]; we could just see the edge of it. Everything we had like dog food buckets and everything blowed away and was lost. It got cold after the gale and ice started making again so after two or three nights we tried it for home. We come up to Adams Point and struck across the Bay to the big shoal. There was a bunch of Innu coming home with us and they got into bad ice at Middle Point; their stuff got in the water but we helped them and everybody got out with all their stuff. We went ashore at Middle Point and made on a big fire and got warmed up and dried out. I remember the Innu had a big bucket of **pemmican** and they made soup with it and shared it all around. We were okay from there on home. We always sent someone ahead to try the ice before we went across it with our dogs. The fella would walk ahead and test the ice with his axe, then he'd wave to us to come on with our dogs and komatiks.

We would meet hunters from Rigolet in the Mealies. The Sandwich Bay people hunted the same herd but from the other side of the mountains. There were always Innu hunting over there, too. There was Michel Pasteen, Shimun Pasteen, Charlie Rich from Davis Inlet and his son Sebastien. Charlie Rich spent the whole winter over there some years. The two Pasteen families often camped in over the Mealies on Fish Lake, the source of Shoal River.

One time over there hunting caribou in the '50s, I believe Bill or Clayton was with me, I got really sick; don't know what it was. I think I had a fever. I was never sicker in my life. Russell Groves and some other fellas were camped there, too, and they gave me Aspirin or some kind of pills but it didn't do any good. Charlie Rich and his wife and another family were there. I think some of Shimun Pasteen's crowd was there, too. We were camped right by them at the foot of the mountain, and Mrs. Rich found out I was sick. In the evening she came in the tent with a quart kettle with some stuff for me to drink for my sickness. It was spruce brush, the fresh tips of the new growth, boiled and boiled; she told me to drink it all and then go to sleep; she told me I would sleep. I put a little sugar in it to make it easier to take, like she said, and then drinked it, thinking it wouldn't do me no good. I drank a little at a time, probably a cup or two, then I crawled in my sleeping bag and did I ever sleep, woke up almost perfect, and soaking wet with sweat; my sleeping bag was soaked with sweat. After a day or two, I was hunting along with the boys again. That was a long time ago. I was only about 17 or 18.

I used to hunt caribou in the Mealies and take them right to Goose Bay. Ossie Michelin always used to get some from me, and a lot of other people who were working on the Base and couldn't go hunting. There was no licence or limits them days. I guided other people down there with my team, people that didn't know the area, young Juddy Blake for one.

I loved caribou hunting. I still do, go whenever I can. We haven't been allowed to hunt in the Mealy Mountains since the late 1960s. We used to go in almost to Parke Lake. The Innu used to be in at Parke Lake and Muskrat Lake; we saw their track lots of times but never met them, knowed they were there. When we got to the edge of the green woods, that was our limit, we came back. We had to take our tent when we went in that far.

I met up with Sebastian Rich in there and hunted with him for three days one time; there was no caribou that time, none. Another time I remember meeting up with Sebastian and their crowd on their way home, hauling caribou out. He had a pair of beautiful beaver tail snowshoes with pretty tassels on them and I told him that I wanted them; I was just getting started hunting and mine were in poor shape. He told me he would sell them to me for 12 dollars and I told him when he got home to go see my mother and get the money from her as I had no money on me and that's what he did. I gave him my old snowshoes. Boy, did I ever take off on those beautiful snowshoes. I hunted with Louie Penashue in the Mealies, too; he could really walk on the snowshoes; I can still see him swinging those snowshoes and going. He was tall and slim and full of energy. I had to run a little sometimes to keep up with him.

I loved it in the Mealies, hunted over there a lot. The Whites from Gutter's Bight trapped that whole shoreline. Hiram White and Sam Broomfield were over there when I first started hunting that area.

I went caribou hunting with Clarence Wolfrey one time. I had a team of seven dogs and he had a good team, too; I think he had six. There were no caribou close that year. I was talking to Clarence and he said he knew the area real good down to the lower part of the Bay, down to English River and Peter Lucy's Brook, 'cause he was from Rigolet. We decided to go down for a caribou hunt. We went down along the south side of the Bay, stayed at Big Point on the way down; next day we went on to English River and when we went to go in the river to get into the mountains, we knew there was a falls there and if we could get over it, we'd be okay. So we tried it but there wasn't enough snow so we had to turn around and come back out again. Then we went further along east to Peter Lucy's Brook; that's right across from the Narrows. The weather was very cold going down; it was in January and we had good going. We got to Peter Lucy's Brook and started hunting from there. There was a house there, an old homestead, and we stayed in that.

We didn't hunt the first day. The second day we walked in with our grub bag and kettle; there was no sign of caribou. We were a long ways from the mountains down there; there's a lot of bog land with little ponds; that's where English River and Peter Lucy's Brook come from. We saw lots of track of people so we knew people had been hunting. When we got in to the caribou grounds, we stopped in the middle of the day to boil the kettle and when we were having our lunch we saw five caribou walking right out on the middle of that marsh. We'd been pretty discouraged 'cause we'd been walking all morning and no sign of caribou. We waited; there was no place to hide ourselves out on the bog so we decided to take a long shot. I had a .2535 rifle and I got three caribou but two got away. Clarence had an old .303 British that they used in the war and it was useless; the bullets didn't go far. We were some glad of our caribou, three big old bald-headed stags, some good eating. We went out to our camp and next day took our dogs in to haul the caribou out. When we were trying to get them out we had to cut a lot of sticks and trees to get them out. We were glad that we only had three. That was the only time I ever hunted off the Mealies, even though it was the same herd.

When we got back out to our camp, there were some fellas there from Rigolet area; we found out it was their tracks we saw. They had beaver traps there all fall and were checking their traps and also their seal nets. They had set seal nets in the pressure cracks in the ice and were getting lots of seals, good dog food. They gave us some; we were some happy, had some for going home, too. They also had seven or eight beaver. That was Frances Campbell and Harvey Mucko and some others.

Going down, I had noticed the ice was kind of bad between English River and Peter Lucy's Brook; the water had soaked up on the old ice, but it was so cold we didn't have a problem. Frances and Harvey told us we'd come over bad ice there and that nobody ever travelled there. Coming home, we crossed the Bay over to Valley's Bight and came along the north shore to around Lowlands, then crossed back over to Big Point. At Big Point there was a radar site being built. It was a DEW Line site but it was never completed. Uncle Piercy Chaulk was the caretaker and we stayed with him in the house there and then came home the next day. Big Point is about 60 miles from North West River. On the way home, one of Clarence's dogs stepped in a crack and broke his leg. I never saw that happen before or since. Now he was short one dog; I think I gave him one of mine for the trip home. As far as I can remember, that was the only caribou we had that year; they were pretty scarce.

I can't remember when we first hunted the George River caribou, but I flew in to Border Beacon for a hunt when I was working with Forestry. That's after they banned hunting in the Mealies. I know I had a snowmobile in '63 or '64 and I hunted a few more years in the Mealies with snowmobile before they closed it for hunting. Once they cut off the Mealy Mountain hunt, that's when we started hunting the northern zone. The only way to get in there was by plane, or when the Churchill Falls road was pushed through, a long snowmobile ride to get in there via western Labrador. We had to have our caribou.

I remember caribou being way in back in the Mealies one time, too far to go on snowmobile; me and Bernard and George Chaulk hired a plane and flew in there for a few days to hunt. We were only allowed to kill stags and it was hard to tell. So if you killed a female, you left it there rather than go to jail. They all got antlers and you can't tell the difference unless you get close enough to see their rear ends.

There was some caribou hunting in on the Red Wine Mountains but I never went in there; I was trapping them times. There was never a resident herd in there, just some stayed behind from the George River herd occasionally. There were a few animals around for a few years.

The first time we went up Grand Lake on snowmobile to hunt the George River herd was after I retired. The caribou we got up there came after the fires in the 1960s and 1970s. It all burned up there, and in 30 years the caribou began feeding on the burn. I was told by officials, many years before that, that it took 60 years before it growed back fully, but the caribou were back there in 30 years for their winter feeding grounds. It might not be growed back fully, but good enough for caribou to find enough food to winter on. The burn provided food for them and that's why they're where they are now. I fought on those fires in the '60s and '70s and remember them well.

In my grandfather's day, they used to hunt the Grand Lake area, too, but that was also after a large burn that happened around 1881, according to HBC journals (Davies, 1963). The trappers all had to leave. They lost their traps, cabins, everything in that fire. My father never killed a caribou or saw a caribou around Grand Lake in his life.

None of the settlers from North West River hunted caribou in the Mealies until the Innu came across the portage from St. Augustine to trade here and told them about the caribou in on the Mealies. They came here and talked about all the caribou and then our people started going over there to hunt. My grandfather only hunted caribou in the Mealies once. I don't remember who was with him but it was the only time he hunted over there. Grandfather used to hunt caribou in back of Watties. My father's caribou hunting was all done over in the Mealies.

They had to close hunting in the Mealies because of hunting pressure, airplanes, helicopters, snowmobiles, all after them. The population went down low. Caribou don't run away from hunters or forest fires. They stand aside out of the way and then go back again. I've seen their tracks in the morning all in among the ashes after a forest fire dies back a bit in the night. They don't run away from jets; they don't know what it is, just a big boom. Caribou will run a little away from hunters and then circle back to feed; they circle constantly. They won't run out of their feeding grounds as long as there's food for them.

Once we got the caribou home, we brought two at a time into the kitchen and thawed them and skinned them in the middle of the floor; then we quartered them up and hung them out in the storehouse; we'd go out and cut off what we wanted to cook for a meal. We butchered them with a knife and an axe, the hard way. We dried some around the stovepipe in the house. We really depended on caribou meat.

I got one in Nipishish one time and dried it in my tilt. God, it was good. That's why I gotta have dry meat now; I get hungry for it. The wolves killed that caribou for me. They drove it out in a pond but they won't fight or kill anything in the water, 'cause they're swimming and can't reach the bottom, but the old caribou stood up real good on his long legs. I went in to my traps and I saw this big lump out in the middle of a small pond; it looked like a big rock but it wasn't there before. The shore of the pond was covered with wolf tracks but the pond wasn't froze enough to walk on. When it froze solid, I walked out to see what it was. It was a big old caribou, hooked on the bottom by the antlers and floating because he was all blowed up. I couldn't get him up but I took all the legs off him. I was some glad for the meat; took it out to the Red Wine River and shared it with my father and Ellis Baikie and them fellers. The meat was perfect. The wolves had the shore tore up waiting for the caribou to come ashore but he stayed there until he died. That's what caribou do when wolves get after them, they head for the water because the wolves can't fight them there. An old caribou has got long legs and he can stand on the bottom. Other than that, I never saw caribou in the Nipishish area until recent years. I saw fresh tracks a few times, but it was heavily wooded country where we trapped and we never saw any unless they were out in the open on a pond or something.

Another time hunting in the Mealies, five of us went over to hunt; there was me and Russell, Bill Michelin, Clayton, and Wilbert. We had a team each. We met some other hunters at Louse Brook and they told us the caribou were so far in that we couldn't do it in one day, we'd have to take our tents and camp in there overnight. We had to go right in to the green woods, almost to Parke Lake. We decided to take a tent and stove between four of us, the bare basics, and that one person would have to stay outside and look after the dogs. We cut the deck of cards to see who would stay behind and tend the dogs and Bill got the low card and stayed behind. We always cut the cards to see who was going to cook the dog food, who was going to make on the fire, who was gonna get water, who was gonna make splits. Juddy Blake was bad for that. He'd always win, too. Bill didn't mind because we were after meat and we did what we had to do. We probably got 25 caribou that trip. We came out and got the dogs, and the next day started hauling them out, two at a time. It took a couple days to haul them all out. We started eating caribou right away, always cooked the breastbone first.

That same time, I got turned around. I thought the boys were going wrong, I thought we were headed for Cartwright. I was cross with them but at last I had to give in; it was hard to do so. The boys knew I was the one that was turned around. We were chasing caribou, running every direction, and I got mixed up; there were lots of caribou in there that time.

Another time, after the Inuit families had been relocated up here from the north Coast, me and Bill Michelin went in Between the Rivers after caribou. The Inuit were hunting over there, and for the first time I saw igloos. I went in one but never slept in it. There were two igloos and the Inuit had them there for when they went over hunting. They had their own teams, built them up after they got here. They didn't know where to hunt, and this was heavily wooded country, so different for them. We were told they were moved up here because they were sick and needed to be near the hospital. We didn't know. If I knew then what I know now, I would have invited some of them to go hunting with me but I thought they were sick and couldn't hunt. Eventually they started hunting and we just thought they must have got well; that should have been set up before they came here so us people here could help them out.

Inuit people from Rigolet came up here and went trapping with my father before my time. He talked about them many times. One was Tommy Kunnok. He trapped with my father for two years at least. Another man that trapped up around the head of Grand Lake was Willie Ikey, from the Rigolet area. Uncle Austin and my father knew him and talked about him a lot. Willie Ikey adopted Charlie [Michelin] Ikey. I hunted caribou in the Mealies lots with Charlie; he knew the Inuit ways. He used to live in Rigolet but moved up to Goose Bay to work on the Base, worked there until he retired. He used to call me from the Valley [Happy Valley] and tell me that he would wait for me over on Adams Point at a certain time and a certain day to go caribou hunting and I'd meet him over there. He always wanted me to go hunting caribou with him. I used to love hunting with him, he was so comfortable and good at everything; he was a good bushman, hard to keep up with; he could get cross quick if anybody crossed him but he was kind to everybody; you always had to go to his tent for lunch. I remember hunting caribou down at Beaver Brook one time and I came along by his tent in the evening and I had to go in; he had caribou cooked for supper for everybody.

One time when we were hunting together, Charlie Ikey wanted a plane. He got a piece of metal from somewhere, probably from some of the old houses that used to be there at Louse Brook where we were camped. He started sharpening it with a file. He worked and worked at it until it was right sharp, then he shaped a block of wood to hold it and had himself a proper plane. I often think about it. I'd love to have it or see it. This was in the middle of winter, coldest kind of weather. He went to a nearby brook and scraped up buckets of mud, brought it back to his camp, and spread it on the metal shoeing of his komatik. He put the mud on and it froze solid, stronger than pure ice. Then he took boiling water and poured over it and smoothed it with the plane and with his hand, made it right smooth, shaped it wider than the shoeing, about five inches or so wide, and real thick. He said you had to be careful not to hit rough ice or it would break off but there was lots of snow that time of year. When he got it done after a couple days, he had us come and try his komatik and it would slide some easy. He said that was what they did up in Fort Chimo area where he used to live. He was married to a woman from up there, and then they moved back to Labrador. Our old metal shoeing wouldn't slide like that at all. We used to use hot water on our metal shoeing to ice it up so it would slip better but it didn't last long. That old metal shoeing, you could hear it grinding on the snow. Today we have plastic shoeing on our komatiks and our snowmobiles haul the komatiks. It's a lot easier these days. I remember when Charlie left for home that time; he had a big komatik with nine caribou on it and about eight or nine dogs in his team. He slipped along right easy.

One time Henry Blake wanted me and Bernard Chaulk to go caribou hunting with him. Henry was 70 years old and still had a dog team, about three or four dogs, well looked after. I put my dogs with his to make up a big team and Bernard had his team. We went over to Louse Brook. I was riding on the komatik with Henry. All the way along he was telling me how the mountains were formed, how the earth was made, how wonderful everything was, kind of like a scientist. When we got to Louse Brook and camped, he told us about a different route in to the mountains he knew of from years before when they lived over at Big Bight. He said we'd go in there and camp and we'd be closer to the caribou if there were any. The caribou were scarce that year.

We met some fellas coming out who'd been there a week and never saw a one. Henry told me and Bernard to go in the old way and he'd go the other way. Bernard and me got in there and we came across a big company of caribou, coming down through a lead; we went up there and waited and killed all we wanted. We come out that evening but Henry still wanted to go in that other route. We went in and helped him carry the tent and stove out and then we hauled all the caribou out with the dogs.

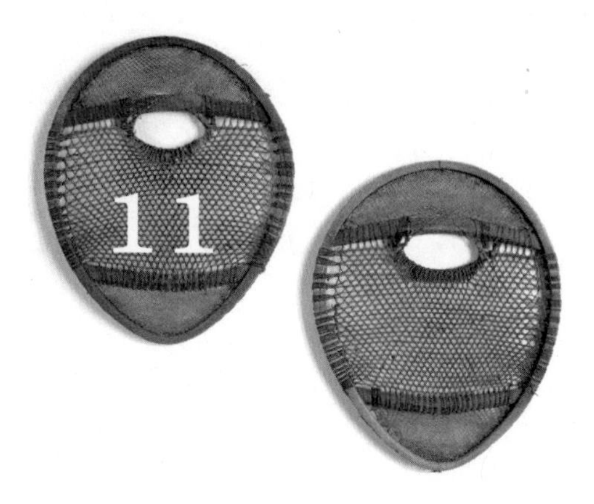


# TRAPLINES AND CUSTOM LAW

There was a custom law back when people trapped for a living. It was made by the trappers themselves. I read that someone helped the trappers set that up around the 1890s; I believe it was some fur traders and A.P. Low that helped them. It was based on traditional knowledge and common sense. The only time I saw any custom law written down was when Wallace McLean had a story about it in *Them Days* (McLean, 1976). I don't think the trappers ever had that law written down.

Local trappers were just trapping close to North West River in a small area. The HBC had workers in service here in the summer and sent their workers off to different areas to trap in the winter and the local people saw them coming back with big piles of fur, valuable furs. Then people started getting the idea to go further away and try to get more for themselves.

Every trapline was on a river that people could get to with canoe; every trapper had a small stretch of river and also a cross-country path; for example, our family had a five- or six-day inland path as well as traps on the river. The custom law said that nobody could set a trap within four miles of another trapper's line. If some trapper came on the river where you had your traps, he would have to go four miles inland clear of yours before he could set traps, or start at the end of your line along the river and go on from there.

Custom law also said that if another trapper set traps on your line, the first time it happened, the trapper who owned that trapline would hang up the other man's traps and let him know that his traps were hung up in a tree. The next time it happened, the traps would be smashed up with an axe, and if that didn't work, if that same trapper kept setting his traps on the other trapper's territory, then all the other trappers in that area would get after him. If that was allowed to continue, it would ruin everybody. You had your own place and nobody dared go on it to trap. To my knowledge, the hanging up or breaking up of traps of someone on your line never happened them days. What was the good of going on someone else's territory? There was barely enough fur in that area for one trapper, let alone two or three. So it was to your advantage to steer clear of other trappers; you'd go as far away as you could from everybody else and have a better chance of getting fur.

Anybody could go on your land to hunt partridge or rabbit, pass through, or stay to [in] the tilts; we all did that. When I started out, you never needed a tent going up Grand Lake. Trapping started from North West River and there were tilts the whole length of Grand Lake and into the Naskaupi River, in every direction. You could make it from tilt to tilt every day. We never even took a tent, didn't need it. If something came up that you couldn't make it to the next tilt, no problem roughing it outdoors for a night or two. Custom law said that you left at least one night's supply of wood at the tilt for the next person.

If you were crossing someone's land and there was an animal in a trap, you would kill the animal if it was live, hang it up, and reset the trap. That happened dozens of times. Between North West River and Red Wine River, there were hundreds of traps along Grand Lake. You could see some of them right from the shore. I knew where every trap was in that 55 miles and who they belonged to. They were all right out to the water's edge and you knew where all the good places were for a trap. I would hang up lots of fur and reset traps on my way along.

These days with people hunting from their trucks along the roads, there's a lot of fur being taken in a small area but no one person is making a living at it; it's just a supplement to his income. Nobody has made a living at trapping for many years. In our time, it was all done on water routes so you were really spread out. These days, people set traps anywhere, with no respect for anyone and certainly not for the animals. I've seen traps set 10 feet from another man's traps; I heard someone say that as long as the trap chains didn't cross, it was okay. That don't make sense. It was different when we were trapping to make a living; we were after every fur we could get and we trapped when the fur was at its best to get the best price. Now it's all changed. Now people don't care if the fur is prime or what price they get, they just want to beat out the other person and get more than they do. It's pure greed and jealousy.

I see traps up in Grand Lake set amongst my traps; I've seen them the first week of October. When I go to set my traps, the fur on my trapline is already caught, even before its prime. Brian Michelin told me the same thing happened on his trapline up at Sand Banks on the Grand River, after the road to Churchill Falls went through and crossed his trapline.

The Newfoundland government made laws about trapping, but how can they make laws about our country when they don't know it? The provincial laws now are about the dates when you can trap. We never set traps until the middle of October, and mink traps not until the first of November. Climate has a lot to do with prime fur times. The trapping times on **the Island** are way before Labrador but Labrador furs, because it's colder here, are prime before Newfoundland furs. Now I can't set traps before the first of November. I wrote three letters to the government about changing the trapping seasons and they listened to me but the next year they changed back, every time. I wanted them to leave them according to the old custom laws, the middle of October except for mink, which would be the first of November. I wanted them to end mink trapping at the end of February, and fox and lynx trapping around the 15th of March; we could go on trapping beaver and muskrat and otter later, because their furs are still good.

There's no use trapping fur when it's not prime; 250 years of trapping showed that. Even now the regulations have trapping season here starting the first of November. The fur is only good for a couple months and then it goes downhill again.

Traplines were sold but the land was never sold. We didn't own the land. You had traps, tilts, maybe even a canoe that could be all sold to another trapper. When people got old or crippled and couldn't go to the country, they would get someone to trap it on shares for them: one-third for the trapper, two-thirds for the owner. The owner fitted the trapper out with everything, traps, tilts, canoe, everything.

Upper Lake Melville area trappers always trapped alone, some for as long as seven months. The ones that went in to the Height of Land, right to the Quebec border, stayed in there for six or seven months because it was too far to come back for Christmas. The ones closer to home were gone for three or four months; they came home for Christmas and then went back again for three or so months. Another reason our trappers trapped alone is because if there was a second man, there was nothing for the second man to do, and you still had to share the money you made and it could cause trouble between them.

Most trappers who went the long distance, like to the Height of Land, trapped until they were 55 or so. They had been working hard on long portages, a month on portages and carrying heavy loads, and were gone long times. They would give up the long-distance traplines and trap a place closer to home. My father said that after the Innu got 45 or 50 years old and had bigger boys to trap and hunt, they didn't work as hard at it. They let the younger men do it.

I remember leaving in the fall of 1949 to go trapping with my father. We were paddling up Grand Lake in the nighttime because there was less chance of wind at night, especially important when you're going along with a loaded canoe. As we paddled along my father told me about the rules of trapping. He went over all those rules I mentioned and then he said, "You know if an Innu sets a trap on your trapline, leave it alone; they can set traps wherever they want to." I asked him why and he said

"Because the Innu belong here." I said, "Well, I belong here, too; I was born here." He told my brother Russell the same thing and we often talked about it; we didn't understand. I often wondered if the first white men who came with the HBC were told that, not to interfere with the Innu who were already here. Anyway, that's what my father's thoughts were and I wondered about that for years. It's clear to me now; this is their land and we intruded. They were good enough to let us use their land. I never heard of Innu setting traps on anybody else's traplines. If they were coming out the portage and found an animal in our trap, they would reset the trap and bring the animal on out to us. They did that all the time. They were really honest.

The trapline I have on Red Wine and Naskaupi Rivers belonged to old Mersai Michelin, who passed it on to his son, Uncle Joe Michelin, who then sold it to my grandfather, Robert Montague, his son-in-law. My grandfather bought it for my father, who wasn't a well person back then and had to have a place closer home and easy to get to. He also had to have someone nearby because of the sickness he had. When my father got old, and I know he was getting sick then, he was still trapping at Red Wine River and I was trapping on the outside half of the Naskaupi, closer to home and easier to get to. Also, you'd see more people out there, like partridge and rabbit hunters. There was good trapping there; I trapped it for years. My father said that we would change. He'd trap out there and I would take over the Red Wine area from him. Red Wine was a better trapping area but hard travel. We changed around in the late '60s, early '70s, when I came back from school in St. John's.

Brian Michelin told me that Uncle Joe Michelin sold the Red Wine trapping grounds to my grandfather for $100, a low price, but big money them days. If somebody new wanted to trap, they had to go clear of everybody else so they didn't overlap. They'd ask around. Ray Cooper, for example, headed in to Seal Lake because there was nobody trapping in there when he wanted to try trapping.

Harvey Goudie said in a story in *Them Days* that most traplines on the Grand River were made by Goudies (Goudie, 1983). There were

Goudies up the Naskaupi; there was Walter, Bill, Allan, and Uncle Arch. Hegrew Lake and Naskaupi River belonged to McLeans. Traplines passed from father to son or other close relatives. Ellis Baikie didn't have a son but passed his on to Lee Baikie, a relative. Ellis bought Hegrew Lake from Gordon McLean and at the same time my father bought the lower half of the Naskaupi from Gordon. I met Gordon McLean down at the store one time and he asked me if my father was home; he said he was going to ask him if he wanted to buy his trapline. Snowmobiles were just coming out and he said he wanted to sell his trapline to buy a Ski-Doo so his boys could bring home the wild meat and haul wood. He sold Hegrew Lake to Ellis for $250 and the lower half of the Naskaupi to my father for $250.

When those traplines were put up there, I don't think the Innu were trapping there; they were further inland. We only saw them in the summer when they came out here to the HBC post. They stayed here to the middle or end of August, then went back in the country again. They went to Seal Lake, Michikamau, and down to Seven Islands and the Gulf of St. Lawrence and back again the next year, but not every year and not all of them. I look at that old Red Wine portage as a railroad with people travelling back and forth, Innu, us fellers, explorers from outside. It had portages branching off in all directions, like to Davis Inlet, Voisey's Bay, and George River and the Ungava Peninsula of Quebec.

I read that the HBC tried to have a priest stay in North West River so the Innu would come out to see him and stay around here; they were very religious, all Catholics. The HBC journal says that the priest left here in 1892 and so did the Innu, shortly after. While the Innu were gone from the area, especially up Grand River, that's when a lot of white trappers moved in, like the Height of Land trappers. Later, the HBC got another priest to stay around North West River. If there was no priest, the Innu weren't coming, and so no fur from them. That's all the HBC was interested in.

One good thing that happened in my time was the settlement of Inuit land claims and the formation of Nunatsiavut self-government in 2005. Our family are beneficiaries and it's been a big help in many ways, especially our hunting rights. We still have to obey provincial government regulations but we have some good rights under it, especially the spring migratory bird hunt. That means a lot to us fellows here [upper Lake Melville area] because it was always a big part of our lives and the meat is important to our diets. I'm very thankful we got those rights back after they were taken away years ago.

# INNU

I remember when Shimun Gregoire first came here from Seven Islands, Quebec. He came to North West River by himself, left his family up at the head of Grand Lake. He came here for supplies and I hauled him and his supplies back up the lake on dog team. There was another fellow with him but I've never seen him since. I was about 14 or 15. Shimun asked my father if anybody here spoke French and my father sent me to take him down to the Thevenets, as they all spoke French. Murdock Broomfield and Roland Goudie also hauled loads up the lake at the same time for other Innu.

Shimun told me about it years later when we were in a tent when we were firefighting. He told me he was lost in the country, didn't know where he was, but he saw all these airplanes going in low and then coming out, rising from the same place. He knew about Goose Bay Air Base so knew he was coming in the right direction; he came to the head of Grand Lake and knew then where he was; he knew that North West River was near Goose Bay. He brought his family to North West River later and stayed here then. I remember a lot of girls in his tent, real young kids; one of his daughters had died before he came out here; he was awful sorry about her; he said she was some smart, could clean deerskins, do everything. Shimun told me that he left Seven Islands because it got too crowded there; it was about the time that the iron ore industry started there.

I remember Charlie Rich coming out from Davis Inlet. He came out on the Red Wine portage the first year I was up trapping with my father, so that was 1949. He could talk English, Inuktitut, and of course, Innu. He camped by us; I'm not sure what time of year it was, but there was ice. He had a big family with him, had some little hunting dogs. He stayed around here but he said there were "too many sticks." I think he meant there were too many trees. He spent a lot of time up at Green Point, on the north side of the Rapids, when he first come here. In the winter, he spent a lot of time in the Mealies, almost lived there, over by Shoal River and Little River, right at the foot of the mountains. Those were good places for caribou and fish.

I also saw Charlie Rich in by **the Biscuit** when I was in there caribou hunting. I don't know what happened to him after that. His son Sebastian was about my age; we worked together at Forestry and I hunted caribou with him in the Mealies. He told me he remembered meeting me up Red Wine River. Simeo, another one of Charlie's sons, stayed here. Tommy Rich was his son, too; I remember him. Charlie was a small little man; he didn't have strong Innu features; his colour was different, too. He was a real chatterbox. I can still hear him, yak, yak, yak. Me and Clayton and Aukie were always talking like him. It was his wife who gave me medicine over in the Mealies.

The Ashinis were up the Naskaupi, too. Squasheen and Joseph, and Danien (Pone) and Anisquash, Edward Andrew's father. Old Otwan, he was my father's best friend, here and in the country. We'd take them up to the Red Wine River Portage in August in our motorboat and see them when they came out to pick up supplies in the winter or when they were heading back to North West River in the spring. Penute Ashini and Matthew Ben were the younger men. They were two fine men. Peter Jack and his family were up there, too. He and my father were good friends. My father liked them all.

Sinabest Otwan, Penute Antuan's father, really helped my father one time. The first fall I went trapping with my father, he got all these boils around his neck and around his waist and they were really sore. We never got our traps set up on the 15th of October because he was so sick, but I couldn't leave him and he couldn't travel; he was just laying around. I had a few small traps set close around the tilt for weasel and the like. Finally, he asked me if I thought I could go in on the hills and set up the cat traps; there were seven. I hadn't been in there before but I knew how to set traps so I went in and got the traps set, tended them a few times, and got a few lynx. There was quite a bit of snow down and I'd see these big rocks covered in snow, big lumps, and think they were bears or something. I was awful nervous at first.

Old Sinabest came out to our tilt at Red Wine River; he was always coming out every week or so from his camp in around Big Otter Lake, just to pick up a few supplies; he'd bring us dried meat or pemmican or something to trade. This time he killed three bears in a cave, a mother and her two young. Sinabest said we could have a bear if we went in with him and picked it up. I asked how long and he said "one day." I figured one day for an Innu would be one week for me so I told my father I wouldn't go. Sinabest always brought some bear meat out to us.

Anyway, Sinabest knew right what to do for my father, just like a doctor. He boiled a big pot of water and set him up and started putting hot cloths on his boils and started squeezing all this stuff out of the boils. In no time at all, my father was better. I didn't know if we should come home when he was sick but he never mentioned it. Sinabest died when they came out of the country one spring. When the Innu came out in the winter, they never camped in their summer place, where Sheshatshiu is now; that's a bad place in the winter, open to northeasterly winds. They camped along Little Lake here or around our houses. In June when they came out, they camped where the community is now.

The Innu would visit us at our homes, have tea and a talk. They'd have dances with big fires on the beach, or sit all day and play checkers; nobody could beat Charlie Rich at checkers. I'd sit and watch them all day, go to their weddings and dances, play football with the other boys; they'd come over here to play football, in on old **Strathcona**'s hayfield, where the ball field is now. In the winter when they came for a week or two, some would camp down by our place or Grandfather's, right down by the river. They were only out for a short time, a week or so.

Father was pretty fluent in Innu, talking about weather and animals and travel; so was my grandfather. The Innu were always at Grandfather's and my father's, drinking tea and smoking, the house right blue with smoke. You'd see a long string of them coming down the lake, then they'd stop at our place for tea and we'd hear all the news from up in the country. They camped by our tilt up there. They didn't carry much, just a pack of tobacco in their pocket, that's all. They'd visit Ellis Baikie and Henry Michelin, too.

The HBC outpost a couple miles inside the mouth of the Naskaupi River wasn't in operation in my time. Uncle Bert Blake used to work around there, getting wood and helping; it would only be staffed in the winter because that's when the Innu would be travelling and unable to get down Grand Lake to the HBC post at North West River. Years later, I remember when my father had supplies up at the Red Wine, for the HBC, things that wouldn't spoil or freeze. Sometimes when we came back from our cross-country trip, the Innu had been there, took supplies, and left some furs. The HBC wanted to keep them coming and bringing their furs.

One time me and my father and Uncle Austin were all in Nipishish. We would travel from our fourth tilt around a big long point to go visit Uncle Austin for a night every few weeks. We'd be all day going there, out in the wind and cold. An Innu man came to our tilt one morning, hardly daylight; Father asked him if he'd been walking all night. He said no, that he had just come from Austin's, that Austin's place was right close. Father could hardly believe him; he kept asking him if he'd walked all night. We went back with him and in an hour, we were at Uncle Austin's. He had cut across that long point. The Innu knew the country so well.

Philip Selma was always in that country. When I was in to Nipishish one time, at the fourth tilt, Philip came to my tilt and I told him I was starting for Red Wine River in the morning. He came back the next morning early and walked out with me. It was a long walk and we were still travelling after dark. It was a pretty moonlight night and we were checking traps along the way; one trap had a big old lynx sitting up in it. I got my gun but Philip told me, "No, not in the dark." He said that he'd kill him with a stick. So he got a stick and walked up to the lynx and the lynx just sat looking at him; he took a swing, and just as he swung, the lynx jumped and he missed him; I heard his stick crack on a tree, and when I looked, Philip was inside the trap house with the lynx outside of him. Philip told me I'd better use the gun. He was coming out for supplies. He had a little bag hung over his shoulder, with some dried caribou meat in it; he'd take a chaw every once in a while and give me a chaw. We boiled the kettle at our second tilt and came on out to the river all in one long day.

I have walked from Nipishish out to the Red Wine River in one day in the fall, 12 hours. I'd leave before daylight and get out late. Another time, my father had sent me to North West River to get supplies. It was December and I came down and back in our little clinker-built rowboat with a 3-horsepower motor on it. I was probably home for a week. When I got back, I walked on the ice from the mouth of the Naskaupi River to the Red Wine River and when I got to our tilt, my father had left a note dated the day before saying that he was gone on our cross-country path to Nipishish and he was going to wait at the first tilt. I had a cup of tea, and went on with my big load of supplies on my back. At the first tilt he left a note that he was gone on to the second tilt, but he wasn't there, either, so I went on to the third and then the fourth tilt to meet him; I got to the fourth tilt at four in the morning. I slept and slept when I got there. I was never so tired in my life. That was probably 30 miles.

Another time, I came out from Nipishish, from Uncle Austin's tilt to our second tilt, straight out, and on out to Red Wine, and there was a note on the stove from Father. He'd just left that morning to go home for Christmas. It was dark and I never even stopped for tea. I headed out the river on the ice and about halfway out I met Innu and I asked them if they saw my father and Ellis; they told me where they were camped and that they couldn't go on because it was blowing too hard on Grand Lake. I went right on and got there at two in the morning. My father had a job to believe I come all that way from Nipishish in one day. He could've done that himself in his young days. He and Ellis were camped on that island at the mouth of the river. They'd been up having a smoke and I could see their candle through the tent. There was open water up that far, kept open by the warmer water in Grand Lake and the current.

We went on the next day to the mouth of the river where Ellis had an 18-foot freighter canoe with a small motor and we hopped in and came on; the slob got too thick so we crossed from Cotter's Point to Burnt Point on the south side; we took some chance crossing the lake; we camped at Burnt Point for the night. Myself and Father had to keep knocking the ice off the canoe with the axe and canoe paddle. I wanted to come on, get home and see the girls, and I would have, but we were on the south side so we camped for the night. We got home next day.

The last Innu people I remember in around Red Wine River was Etien Rich and Michel Jack and their extended families. They were at Muskrat Lake on Crooked River, halfway to Nipishish. Their two families were camped there; they'd come out Red Wine to visit us, hear the news, and pick up some grub if we had some extra. From our second tilt, if it was a clear day and the wind right, we could hear their dogs barking. In the fall when I was trapping on the lower part of the Naskaupi, Etien and Michel came from North West River with some supplies and they stayed with me at my tilt one night. They were on their way back to Muskrat Lake; their families were in there. They saw I had some #1 small traps and they wanted to exchange them for some bigger double-spring traps; that's all they could get at the HBC and they wanted lighter ones because they had to carry them; so we traded. The next morning they got in their canoe and went on.

We'd see them together all the time. They went up to the Red Wine Portage and went in from there; a path branched off from our first tilt down to Muskrat Lake; they took their canoe with them; that was nothing them days, to pick up a canoe and go on. Michel Jack was a real good hunter; he had good duration on snowshoes; he could go all night. They hunted up around Nipishish and out towards White Bear Lake. There was a resident herd of caribou in the White Bear Mountains but they got wiped out. Peter Jack was good at building canoes; Joseph and Squasheen were all good at that and making snowshoes too. Etien was a good carpenter. He helped Jim Michelin build part of my house here, just using a hand saw and hammer and second-hand lumber.

Innu around here never had dog teams, they had little small **crackies**; sometimes they'd harness them up to their sleds. I remember one time, there was a crowd of Innu coming down the lake and the head feller had about five or six little crackies harnessed up to a sled and he was hauling, too. I kept my dogs going straight so they wouldn't pass too close to them but when we got up to them, my dogs made a dart for the little crackies; buddy got them to one side and gathered all the traces together in his hand and threw his little dogs over his shoulder in a bundle and walked on, looking back at me. The women coming along behind were laughing some hard.

# MUSIC, FIDDLE PLAYING, AND MEMORIES OF FIDDLERS

There was fiddle music as far back as I can remember. First time I ever remember hearing a fiddle played, I was perhaps three or four years old. Uncle Joe Broomfield used to play and he had three or four sons, Murdock, Clifford (Notie), and Calvin, that played, but the one I remember most was Murdock. I liked the fiddle right from day one. Fiddle music was our music here; there was nothing else, no guitars, but there were a few mandolins around; I could play the mandolin. Murdock Broomfield had one. I guess they got theirs from their ancestors that came from Scotland.

It wasn't like out on the Coast or on the Island where there were accordions. The Inuit on the Coast would buy or trade accordions with the Newfoundland fishermen. We're 120 miles inland, so the fishermen never came in here. For our dances we only danced to fiddle music and if we couldn't get a fiddler, it was the mouth organ; always somebody could play that. Murdock Broomfield was always around with my father; he lived near us; I heard him and watched him play the fiddle. Uncle Pleamon [Philemon] Blake was a good fiddler. He used to play for the dances and us kids would be outside listening around the windows; we was always hanging around the dance hall when there was music going on; that's where the excitement was. I was only seven or eight years old then.

Later on, Murdock found out I liked the fiddle and I used to go down to his house and try it out, try to play it like him. At last I could pick out a tune. Later on, he loaned me his fiddle for a while. I think I had it for a whole winter. I was probably 12 or 14 then, so I picked up a lot. When Uncle Pleamon and Uncle Joe saw that I liked the fiddle, they started teaching me, too. I used to go to Murdock's house a lot and Uncle Pleamon's and they'd show me chords. I guess they saw a potential in me and I was very interested. Uncle Pleamon always had the homebrew on the go and he'd give me some, even before I was drinking age. We'd go in the living room and he'd show me how to hold the fiddle, where to put my fingers, and then he'd pass it over to me and tell me to do it and then tell me if I was doing it right.

Uncle Plea always sat the same way, with his knees together, always had deerskins with khaki leggings sewed on to them; I never forgot that. He loved having people around. He was a really nice man. He liked music and lively times. He used to come up to Uncle Austin's a lot. He had an awful round nose, like an Innu, and he said that was good for tipping up the glass of homebrew, his nose fit right in the glass. I don't know if my parents knew I was at the homebrew.

Uncle Pleamon was an excellent carpenter; built his own house, a wonderful house for them times. He built a lot of houses for other people, too. He trapped up at Watties, had a nice big tilt there. He used to trap inland from Watties; he had a couple tilts in there, too; then he'd come out on Berry Head Brook and walk down along the shore along by his brother Sid's trapping place, to Watties. His son Harold and Harold's wife Sybil trapped there in later years on that same path; they had a beautiful tilt at Watties. The first couple years I was trapping with my father we would stop there on our way home. One time, Harold was gone to the traps but Sybil was there. She gave us a big feed, a big lunch. I remember one morning we got there and she had killed two otters in the brook at Watties.

All the HBC clerks and managers came from Scotland and a lot of these people brought fiddles and their music with them, and that's how the fiddle got here, I found out later. The music we play has lots of Scottish tunes in it and that's the same all across the North wherever the HBC went. Our music is similar to that of the French posts and HBC posts all across Canada, and very different from the Irish-influenced Newfoundland music.

I played for dances for a while but when I got married and started a family, I give it up for 15 years or so; I didn't have time. I never had a fiddle of my own until a few years ago; I just borrowed one. There was none to buy here in the first place and even if there was, I couldn't afford one. There were six or seven fiddles here in North West River. Winton Blake was a good fiddler. He could play piano, guitar, and mandolin, too.

All the other music came when the Base came to Goose Bay, when all the outside people came in, both the military and the civilians. At one time there were 30,000 or 40,000 people here and the instruments came with them: fiddles, guitars, mandolins. There were armed forces men from New Brunswick, Rangers they were called, and they had a four-man band; they used to play for dances down here; the head fiddler was Billy Dixon. Billy Dixon — I'll never forget him and his playing. They played fiddle, guitar, banjo, and mandolin. They loved coming to North West River; they were in a kind of family setting when they come down here. They came down every weekend there was a dance unless the weather or the roads was bad; there was no proper roads them days. They came down on the road that McNamara built to haul gravel to Goose Bay from down here.

Mother played the organ; she used to play at church and she knew all the hymns. She also played these same fiddle tunes on the organ; that's why I play them 'cause I heard them from the earliest days, probably even before I was born since Mother had an organ before I was born. My father loved fiddle music. I remember him talking about Peter Michelin from Sebaskashu playing "The Flowers of Edinburgh" on fiddle; he liked that one awful well. I was told that Grandfather Montague could play the accordion but I never saw him do it. He loved music, was always singing cowboy songs.

Every Sunday we got up and had breakfast, then we'd get cleaned up and around 10 or 11, we'd have almost like a service if there was no minister around. Mother would play the organ and Father would sing; he was considered quite a good singer and he knowed all the hymns. He loved singing "When the Roll Is Called Up Yonder." Mother's organ came from Germany. I often heard my parents talking about it; it had German writing on it but we didn't know what it said. My sister Jane said they bought the organ from old Mr. Budgell in Rigolet. It had pedals, a beautiful organ. I don't know where Mother learned to play and I never thought to ask her; that was a big mistake; now I'm sorry I never asked. Mother played by note and by ear and she could write the notes. She wrote down the notes for a lot of them old trapper songs. She had to learn from somebody, but I don't know who.

The first radio my father owned had earphones; only one person could listen at a time, all crackling and banging; it wasn't very clear. Grandfather had a big radio and listened to all the news and then he'd tell everybody else the news. We listened to country and western music from Wheeling, West Virginia; we'd stay up all night listening to it, also Don Messer and His Islanders, and a station from New Brunswick; everybody would be crowded around listening to the radio. When televisions first came out, Uncle Selby and Aunt Pearl had one; we'd all crowd in to watch Don Messer; their small house was packed full with everybody waiting for Don Messer to come on.

I played for dances for a while when I was 17 or 18. I played fiddle by myself, no guitar player because there was no guitars; that came about later. Our Montague family is right full of music; most all can play something and sing, too. We played the reels and the jigs, fast music, like we play now. There was no waltzing; it was all square dancing. I never saw anybody waltzing until the late 1950s or '60s when I got married. There was lots of step dancing. Mark Mesher and Sandy Riche were good step dancers, so was Oscar Michelin, and lots of others.

I had a band one time. I was probably 18 or 19. We played in the armed forces clubs in Goose Bay. I played fiddle and there were two guitars; Gordie Rendell used to play with me sometimes and there was a young Broomfield boy. The Canadian clubs were mostly all square dancing; the Americans brought in their own entertainment people. Russell played guitar; Stewart, Mike, Tom, and Irv, all of us played guitar, but none of our sisters played. The boys are good at it. We play together now for events. Our cousins Lester and Aukie and Eric play fiddle, too. Uncle Austin's whole family can play, the boys and Shirley and Ray, and the next generation, too. There are a couple younger fiddle players around now; there's Ray's son Craig, and Irv and Mike play fiddle, and Shirley, all Montagues. Mother was very musical, as I said, and so was Aunt Florrie's [wife of Uncle Austin] family, the Flowers from Rigolet. In 2011, our Montague family released a CD of fiddle music and other tunes.

I never sang in public but I sang on the trapline, sang all day long, paddling my canoe, keeping time with the stroke; I sang country and western music, always humming and half whistling. People that don't have music in their heads, I don't know what's in there, what do they think about all day, if there's no music there? That's only me. I'll be working around the house or outside, then I'll come in, sit down and pick up my fiddle, play a few tunes, then go back to my smoke and coffee or work. I'm always at it.

We have a different fiddling style now, different than Uncle Joe Broomfield and them, same finger moves but more what we call a French-Canadian style. The music I heard on the radio back then was called French-Canadian, now they call it Métis. I hear it now on radio and TV, on **APTN**. The Métis across northern Canada are wonderful fiddle players. They heard the music from the same crowd as us, the HBC crowd.

Me and Aukie wrote a song called "Me and Aukie and Grampa." When he was getting old and his mind was going, Grandfather's mind was on trapping and the old days. He used to tell us stories. He told me and Aukie he was going to take us up across the country to Kaipikok River. We were some glad, never heard tell of Kaipikok River before, but we were game to go. We were gonna go up Grand Lake with Grandfather, up Red Wine Portage, and then strike off north, canoe, lock, stock, and barrel, for what we called the spring hunt. We were gonna set traps along the way and pick up a scattered mink. When the spring runoff started, we would go out to the post at Postville and wait a few days, then jump on board the *Kyle* and come home. We`d pay the captain in muskrat skins and head on out the Bay to home. We was some excited, didn't know where we was going, but what an adventurous trip that was going to be. We were gonna pack up and be gone a couple of months. Grandfather was pretty happy when we volunteered to go with him. We were only about eight or nine years old. Aukie is a bit older than me. Grandfather was over 70 years old when he was talking about that trip.

Me and Aukie would be up setting our rabbit snares and working on that song. Another verse was about when we were getting on the *Kyle*, throwing our stuff aboard, and our old black kettle rolled out of our bag and the captain said "what's that?" Every move Grandfather made, we was always laughing at him. He always thought he was striking up his traps. Of course, that had been his life. Ben Best told me he laughed and laughed when he heard that song on the radio. He knowed nobody was gonna do that. The song went something like this:

Me and Aukie and Grampa
We got our minds made up,
We're going to Kaipokok River,
If Grampa don't give up.
We're going in for beaver,
Otter and muskrat I think,
We'll set our traps along the shore
And catch a scattered mink.

Now Grampa said to Louie,
I think we'll go and boil,
We'll take our grub and kettle,
And go on board the *Kyle*.
Grampa said unto the boss,
To see what he had to pay,
He gave the captain sixteen rats,
And headed out the bay.

I remember part of another verse, wish I could remember it all. It goes:

> When we got to Point a Kabou,
> The captain put us off.
> We got in our canoe and said
> "Good-bye" to Kaipokok.

We used to sing that song when we were partying and it kind of took off. It got put in the songbook that the School Board put out [*Songs of Labrador* (Borlase, 1993)].

Murdock Broomfield, the fiddler, used to make a lot of trips up the lake taking supplies for the Innu. Murdock trapped Crooked River and he had a little tilt by us. Murdock would come down from Red Wine River, go across the portage and go in to his traps and back the same day. Uncle Duncan McLean had a little tilt there on the edge of the burn. Uncle Duncan used to cross the river and walk up on the south side and cross the river up there where it was easier to get across. One time when he come to his little tilt, it was gone. He looked across the river and seen a tilt over on the other side where there had never been one before. I don't know what he did that night because he never had a tilt to sleep in but the next day he walked back to his tilt at the mouth of the river; he met Murdock and told him his tilt was gone. Murdock said he knew; he'd towed it across the river in the fall just like they talked about.

Well what a fuss!! Uncle Duncan was some cross. Murdock had said that if the tilt was on the other side, it would be good for both of them and Uncle Duncan agreed with him but never thought he would move it, and then forgot about it. Uncle Duncan made him tow it back. He told everybody he thought he'd seen it all now. They stayed together that night and Murdock said all night long, Uncle Duncan would roll over in his sleep and mumble that he'd seen it all, heard it all now. Murdock said he had some job taking it all apart again, booming the logs over, paddling against the current to get up river far enough so he could put it back in the same place. Murdock had told Uncle Duncan that he moved the tilt, but he wouldn't believe him, said nobody would do such a thing. He thought Murdock was just talking, tormenting him.

I remember them telling about another time over at Kenamu, when a plane crashed in back and that night two fellers showed up to Murdock's tent where he was fishing. They had walked away from the plane crash. They had a bottle of rum and little did they know but Murdock was right in his glee. Murdock told them he would row them down to Kenemish to Uncle Duncan's because he had a motorboat and could bring them back over to Goose Bay. That night, Murdock and the airmen took off in his rowboat, and got to Kenemish early in the morning, and knocked at Uncle's door. Uncle Duncan came out mad and Duck [Murdock] was so excited he couldn't get across what he wanted but they finally got it figured out. Uncle Duncan used to tell about it; he said Murdock was always doing something to him. He said he was so mad, he towed Murdock in the house to hammer him but he couldn't do a good job of it because he only had one hand to work with; his other hand was busy holding up his drawers.

# LATER YEARS

I married Ruth Andersen from Nain. Her father was Waldo Andersen from Nain and her mother was Lillian Voisey from Voisey's Bay. Ruth was the oldest in her family, with brothers Sam [married Mary Sillett] and Norman [married Elizabeth Angnatak], and sister Gladys [married Ray Best]. A younger brother John was raised by the Fords in Nain, and died in a car accident as a young man while attending university in Newfoundland. Sam worked for years as an interpreter and was fluent in several Inuit dialects. He was president of the Labrador Inuit Association in its early years. Norman worked with fisheries and still lives in Nain. Ruth's parents and siblings were all fluent in Inuktitut and Ruth could speak some Inuktitut as well. Her father was a fisherman and trapper and died quite young.

I met Ruth in Nain in the early '50s when I was working as a helper on the Mission plane, pumping floats, scraping ice, all those things. We would fly as far north as Hebron and then back to Nain. One time we stayed overnight at Nain and I went to a dance and met Ruth. Another time I met her on the dock at Nain and just said "Hello" and then never saw her again until she moved up to Goose Bay.

Ruth had worked at the hospital and for Reverend Peacock, the

Moravian minister, in Nain, and then they moved up here for her mother to work at the Grenfell Mission as a cook. Her father had died when she was 11 and her mother was working to support the family. Ruth worked in Goose Bay in the laundry on the Base, and as a cook for Wheeler Airlines.

We got married in Happy Valley at the Moravian Church in December 1958. Ruth was seven days older than me. We had a family of six children, Diane, Peggy, Janice, Brent, Jeff, and Terry. We always lived in North West River except for a couple years in Goose Bay when I had to move up there for work, but I couldn't wait to move back to North West River. Ruth stayed home and looked after the children all through the years. After I retired, she upgraded and got her high school diploma through the College [College of the North Atlantic in North West River]; she'd gone to school in Nain but there was no grades and then she started working quite young. After finishing her high school, she took courses to be a homecare worker and worked at that for years and retired when she was about 60. She was always wanting to learn new things and try new things. She did a lot of volunteer work in the community, too, as a helper in the school and with Girl Guides and the library and the craft shop.

Ruth could do all kinds of sewing; she made a lot of the Grenfell cloth parkas and did beautiful embroidery work on them. She made tents for me and for other people. She made a lot of tablecloths with the Labrador-style embroidery on them and sold them to the Dutch and German armed forces people who came through here. She made clothes for the children and made or fixed all my trapping clothes and other things I needed. I used to dress caribou hides in the style of the Innu and she made moccasins and mitts from the smoked hides for me and for the craft shop. Ruth and I worked on crafts together; I would make things from wood and she would paint them or make clothes for the figures I made. Her mother was a great sewer, too; she made sealskin boots and mitts until she got older and then she did a lot of knitting. Mrs. Andersen lived with us and then, later, with her other daughter, Gladys.

We used to do a lot of camping, took the children and camped in Grand Lake in the fall around Berry Head, and down around the Islands in the spring and down to Mulligan, too. Aunt Maud and Uncle Byron Chaulk loved it when we brought the children down to Mulligan. One time we were camped at the Rapids in the spring and Diane was just little, playing out on the bank, and then we couldn't find her. There she was, tumbled down the bank, and sitting there playing amongst the driftwood sticks, happy as could be.

Ruth loved being outdoors, picking berries and camping. She was a great berry-picker and made all the jams and syrups, and baked good stuff from the berries. She bottled a lot of meat and fish over the years. If she didn't know how to do something, she'd call people and find out how to do it. She liked to cook and she was a wonderful cook. When her mother lived with us, she would look after the older children, and Ruth and me and Jeff and Terry would go up the Naskaupi River at trapping time while I set up my traps.

The last few years before we knew she had cancer, Ruth found it hard to get around and didn't want to go anywhere. We didn't know at the time what was wrong. She was diagnosed in December of 2000 and died in October 2001. I remember her watching the 9/11 events on TV and then turning it off and saying she didn't want to watch any more; it hurt her too much. She lived to see her first great-grandchild and was so proud. She loved making quilts and things for the grandchildren and loved having them visit. She was a great reader, too, loved reading, when she wasn't sewing.

It was some hard being on my own after she died. She had me spoiled and then I had to learn how to do for myself. My children helped me a lot and I learned how to do housekeeping. I always was used to cooking for myself on the trapline; still cook all the wild meats and use a machine to make my own bread. Once in a while I make sourdough pancakes like my father did — some good with jam.

I eventually got into wood-carving as a way to pass the time. I'd always been making things I needed from wood but this was different; now I was doing it as a craft. I make things from wood that I have seen or used all my life. While I work at wood, I think about the old days and all the people who were around then. Sometimes I'll call Bernard or Wilbert to ask them if they remember a certain person or who was related to who.

I get a lot of requests to make dog teams. I put the team all together, harness them and all, just like I used to. It takes an hour of solid work to make one dog but I take breaks in between. I have to saw the wood and get it ready, then saw the shape of the dogs out and carve them using a knife as much as possible; that keeps the dust down, only makes chips. Then I start on them with the rotary tool; then, when I get the rotary tool work done, I have to sand them by hand and then use the rotary tool to put in their eyes and ears and curl their tails; then I harness them and stick them in place on a plaque, tie them into the bridle and hook the bridle to the komatik, and that's about it with the dogs. Now that's only the dogs; then there's the komatik, the snowshoes, the gun, the axe; they all have to be carved out and then lashed to the komatik. Then there's the feller, the driver; that's a lot of work, too. I can do two in about one day, three or four hours for one; there's a lot of work, a lot of sanding, and grinding and cutting and shaping. I make the face to set in. It's a lot of work, too. And he's gotta have a whip; I make it from waxed sinew, also make my lash line from that. Once it's stuck on the plaque, that's about it.

When you're doing craft work, if you want to make a bunch for sale, you don't stop. If you stop for even a couple hours, you don't get ahead. I work eight or nine hours a day when I'm at it. When I sell my crafts I only make three or four dollars an hour; when you consider wear and tear on tools and take that out, it's less than that. You gotta have expensive tools set up, deal with the dust, be cleaning your workshop all the time; there's a whole lot of work to it. You can never get rich on it, but it might help you buy a carton of cigarettes once in a while.

I do it because I need something to do, a pastime. I'm continuously learning, how to use a tool, how to shape something. I always loved working at wood. I even enjoyed cutting firewood when I was younger, go out and make a good path, go out every morning and head into the old wood path, boil the kettle, fool around at that in the middle of the day and then come home with a good day's work done, feel good, sleep good. I'm the same way now, even though I just sit there and carve; it's not hard work but it's time-consuming.

There's a lot to learn about wood. You don't just pick up any old stick of wood and carve something; it's gotta be a special piece of wood. At first when I started, I had no saw to rip wood; I would get a big junk of wood and split that big piece of birch or poplar with my axe; it would split into all different shapes and then you could see shapes in the wood when you were splitting it; then I would choose the piece I was going to use. Some pieces were good for bows and arrows, others were no good. Now I saw my wood, local wood. I cut it in the spring, take it home and saw it into boards, and let it season over the summer; you have to keep a year ahead. You can't work with wet wood; it has to be perfectly dry. I tried drying it in the oven and that works good; microwave didn't work good, though, the sap boiled out, just like blood or grease boiling out of meat. Trouble was, I didn't have a plate under it and I made a bad mess. I did a lot in the oven starting out, small pieces of birch or aspen and it worked real good, dried out quick. Now I don't have to do that, I let it dry outdoors and keep a year ahead.

I learned a lot about doing crafts, looked at how things were made, learned by trial and error. I had an interest. After I retired, I bought a bunch of tools, made some patterns, tried everything. It was rough at first. I burned up a lot of tools, broke a lot of knives. For a while I thought the only one who was going to make money at it was the company that made Band-Aids.

You gotta know how to cut wood. If you're cutting with the grain, it's easy and smooth, but if you go across the grain, it's a different story. You're always watching for that. All in all, I can't find a better thing to do. Trouble is, I might be into it too deep — don't get nothing else done.

I've made a lot of komatiks in my time; still make them if I need them. A komatik has to be strong, stronger now that they're pulled by snowmobiles. You need a good bevel on the runners. We used to tie the bars on with line, used no nails; every bar was individually tied on; that gave the komatik flexibility when you were going over rough ice and snow. Now with snowmobiles, you nail them on. With snowmobiles we go so fast, the line would rub off in no time. Instead of going three miles an hour with dogs, you go 30 miles an hour and the komatik bumping and banging. The nails will hold it okay. We would put the metal shoeing on with screws; you could buy it with the holes for the screws already in it. Now we use plastic shoeing and screw that on.

In dog team days, a good size for a komatik was about 12 feet because we had to sit on it, but now 10 feet is a good size with a box on it. Our dog team ones had a grub box tied on to sit on and everything else was tied on, too. Now nobody sits on the komatik. With a 10-foot komatik you can take five or six caribou. I always make a little compartment at the back for gas in case your can breaks open, so it doesn't get on your stuff.

I make sleds with a man and a dog hauling it; I travelled like that and it wasn't easy. Once the snowmobiles came out, I chucked all that away. Now it's all gone. I did a lot of snowshoe travel, too; I also made snowshoes and sold them; now I make small snowshoes for ornaments. Everything I make is stuff I used, dogs and komatiks, and all the tools and equipment. When I'm carving, I think about them days; I feel like I'm out there, still doing things I loved; I never knowed it was hard them days because I never knowed anything else. I never had no money for nothing so I made it myself, whatever I needed. Now I have the memories.

APPENDIX 1:

# TYPICAL DAY ON THE TRAPLINE

In the fall of the year, you would get up an hour or two before daylight and be ready to start out as soon as it was light enough to see the traps. You had to take advantage of the shorter days, about six or seven hours of daylight, at that time of year. You'd eat your breakfast of leftover meat from the night before, some flummy, lots of tea and, of course, have a smoke. You'd get your grub bag ready, check your gun, snowshoes, axe, and bait for that day.

You would travel about 10 or 12 miles in a day if you were returning to the same tilt, or go about seven or eight miles if you were going to the next tilt on your trapline. You would check about 20 or 30 traps, depending on how close together they were. You would stop for lunch around mid-day. For lunch you'd have flummy and tea and a smoke. If you had any luck with fur, you would skin a larger animal or two while you were stopped in order to lighten your load. That would be lynx, fox, beaver, or wolf, depending on what you got, if any. Then you would either return to your tilt or go on to the next one before it got dark.

In the evening there was lots of work to do. First thing was to make on a fire and get your supper on to cook because you'd be starving. Often there would be a skinned rabbit or plucked partridges left hanging up in the tilt from your last visit, and they would go right into the pot. You might have got a beaver or lynx that day in your traps and put a meal of that on for supper. When your meat was almost cooked, you'd add some rice. You'd make sure you had enough wood on hand for the night and for when you returned.

After supper, you would make your flummy for the next day, then while it was cooking, skin and clean your fur and put it on stretching boards to dry overnight. If you had no fur, you went to bed early. If you had lots of fur, you kept working until it was all skinned and cleaned, and then went to sleep on your bearskin. We would wake up in the night when the fire died down and we got chilly, reach out and shove some more wood in the stove, and then go back to sleep. What a good sleep we would have, we were so tired. The tilts were so small, you could reach everything from one place. We left a boiler and a frying pan at each tilt but carried everything else we needed with us.

Next day would be the same routine. You were always excited to see what might be in your traps, could hardly wait to get to the next one. It would take five days to get around to all your traps, depending on weather and travel conditions. On Sunday, you'd stay around your main tilt, get some wood, do some mending, have a wash and shave, wash some clothes, and have a nap if there was time. At the main tilt, you would place all the cleaned and skinned fur on stretching boards, and let it dry overnight. While at the main tilt we would make yeast bread and sourdough for pancakes; we'd add molasses or raisins to our stove cake, and maybe have some jam, little special things that we didn't carry on the trapline with us.

Sundays were also the days for meeting up with other trappers who might be nearby, hearing the news, or passing on letters from home. We were never allowed to trap or hunt on Sunday [an accepted custom that later became provincial law]. Mostly we were waiting for the day to pass so we could get going again.

APPENDIX 2:

# SUPPLIES FOR THE TRAPLINE

Flour — 150 pounds for 3 months
Tea
Butter
Sugar*
Lard
Powdered milk
Coffee
Salt pork
Salt & pepper
Baking powder
Baking soda
Tobacco
Molasses
Raisins
Rice
Fish net
Fish hooks
.22 cartridges
Rabbit snare wire
Few candies
Yeast for bread and sourdough at main tilt

*Extra sugar was taken for making jam and syrup from berries picked along the trapline. Berries could be picked until covered by snow and kept well. Redberries and squashberries made delicious jam and syrup to be spread on stove cakes or used on flapjacks or sourdough pancakes.

APPENDIX 3:

# TRAPPER'S TILT

The trapper's tilt was built and used only for overnight stops along the trapline. Tilts were built one day's walk apart, about seven or eight miles. The tilt was constructed completely of round logs, roof and all. It was about eight feet square, and six or seven feet to the peak of the roof. The logs for the tilt were all cut on site. The logs were notched with an axe and fitted together with moss between them for insulation. No nails were used.

The roof was covered with birchbark if available; otherwise, fir branches would do a fair job if placed thick enough. Fir branches had to be replaced throughout the trapping season since the brush would dry out from the heat of the stove. Sometimes, trappers took light canvas with them to use on the roof or canvas that bears had stripped off old canoes was used on the roof.

The tilt was equipped with a small homemade galvanized tin stove, which kept the trapper warm after a hard day's walk and was used for cooking his food. Usually a boiler and a frying pan were left at the tilt but nothing else. The trapper kept all his gear with him and carried it on his back from tilt to tilt.

The main tilt on a trapline was usually on the main water access and was somewhat larger.

# GLOSSARY

**APTN:** Aboriginal Peoples Television Network, established in 1999 as a national television network; originally Television Northern Canada, launched in 1992 with over-the-air access only in Canada's North.

**Aunt and Uncle:** Used as terms of respect for older non-related people, as well as for relatives.

**barricade:** Bivouac; temporary outdoor shelter; sometimes called spending "a night in the ashes."

**Bay, the:** Lake Melville.

**bellycatters:** High ridges of ice along the shoreline, formed in the late fall by repeated splashing of water and build-up of ice; many variations in spelling.

**Biscuit, the:** A high round hill in the Mealy Mountains that can be seen from a great distance; used by hunters as a marker in bad weather.

**booms:** Rafts of logs; about 25 or 30 logs of firewood (each eight or nine feet long, the biggest logs in the pile) were tied with rope end to end to form a circular enclosure into which the remaining firewood (200 or more logs) was tossed, then towed home behind a motorboat.

**bottle-nosed diver:** Local name for a sea duck, the surf scoter.

**brin bags:** Burlap bags.

**Brinex:** The mineral exploration arm of the parent company Brinco (British Newfoundland Development Corporation), which developed the Upper Churchill power project.

**browse:** Beavers' winter food supply, stored by their lodge; includes poplar, willow, alders, birch, and spruce.

**bull birds:** Common dovekie, a sea bird.

**burn:** An area that has been burned over by a forest fire.

**Cabot, William Brooks (1858-1949):** American adventurer who made trips to northern Labrador between 1899 and 1910 and travelled with Innu, took photos, and wrote extensively about his adventures, notably in *In Northern Labrador* (1912).

**capelin:** Small forage fish of the smelt family found in the Atlantic and Arctic oceans.

**carries:** The loads carried on a portage; usually four loads per portage, plus the canoe.

**cat:** Lynx or mountain cat.

**catamaran:** Homemade sled with runners to keep the load above the snow.

**clew up:** Wind up; finish; complete; close up.

**clinker-built:** Overlapped wooden clapboard-style construction for a boat.

**Coast, the:** The coast of Labrador, either north or south of Lake Melville.

**come-along:** Hand-cranked winch, fastened to a solid object such as a tree, used for hauling heavy objects.

**CNR boat:** Canadian National Railways-operated coastal boat.

**crackies:** Small mixed-breed hunting dogs, most often used by the Innu.

**deadfall:** Blow-down; a tree that has been blown down by the wind.

**DEW Line:** Distant Early Warning Line; a system of radar stations constructed across Canada's Far North in the 1950s to detect incoming Soviet bombers during the Cold War and to warn of any land-based invasion. The DEW Line is commonly referred to as the radar system constructed across northern parts of Canada; in fact, however, there were three lines: the Pinetree Line, at about 50° North, the Mid-Canada Line, at 55° North, and the DEW Line, along the Arctic coast above the Arctic Circle. The radar line that Louie Montague refers to as the DEW Line was, in fact, the Mid-Canada Line, with most stations completed in eastern Canada by early 1957. This line remained operational until the mid-sixties, when improved Soviet military technology left only the radar installations along the Arctic coasts of the US, Canada, and Greenland of any functional value.

**dickie:** Pullover hooded parka, usually made of canvas or other thin material, worn over heavier shirt or sweater.

**Dorm, the:** Dormitory in North West River for schoolchildren from the Coast; run by the International Grenfell Association.

**doters and rangers:** Harbour hair seals; a doter is the mother and a ranger is the young one.

**duffel:** Thick felted wool, used for coats and liners in boots and moccasins.

**emmett:** Ant.

**Erlandson, Erland (1790-1875):** HBC clerk who was the first European to travel overland from Hudson Strait (Ungava Bay) to the Atlantic coast, in 1834.

**fast ice:** Solid ice that is not broken into pans or floating.

**fathom:** Measurement of water depth; one fathom equals six feet.

**fit out:** Outfit; supplies for the trapline, usually credited by the HBC and subtracted from value of furs when traded.

**flummy:** A flat bread made by trappers from flour, baking powder, salt, and water; sometimes called flummydum or stove cake; called *innu-pakueshikan* or bannock by Innu.

**Grand River:** First called Miste Shipu by the Innu; later called Grand River by trappers; more recently called the Hamilton or Churchill River; the mouth of the Grand River is at Happy Valley-Goose Bay.

**Grenfell Mission:** The International Grenfell Association, started by Wilfred Grenfell; provided medical services to northern Newfoundland and Labrador.

**grub box:** Container for carrying food for travel.

**HBC:** Hudson's Bay Company; sometimes jokingly called Here Before Christ.

**Height of Land:** Elevated plateau of western Labrador forming the head of the Atlantic drainage system and part of the Labrador-Quebec boundary.

**Height of Landers:** Trappers who trapped above Grand Falls, now called Churchill Falls, at the Height of Land in western Labrador near the Labrador-Quebec border.

**Hubbard, Leonidas (1872-1903):** An American adventure writer who attempted to travel from North West River to Ungava Bay via the Naskaupi and George rivers in 1903 with two companions, Dillon Wallace, a New York lawyer, and George Elson, a Métis (Scots-Cree) guide from the James Bay region; they took the wrong route and turned back; Hubbard died of exhaustion and starvation on the return trip. Wallace, meanwhile, published an account of the adventure, *The Lure of the Labrador Wild* (1905), which seemed to cast blame for the failed trek on Hubbard.

**Hubbard, Mina (1870-1956):** Wife of Leonidas Hubbard who, in 1905, with several companions, including George Elson, set out from North West River and successfully completed the trip her husband had attempted. At the same time, Dillon Wallace set out on a similar trek, but Mina accomplished the adventurous journey more quickly and created valuable maps that were included in her book, *A Woman's Way through Unknown Labrador* (1908), in which she sought to exonerate her late husband for the earlier failed exploration.

**ice driving:** Loose pans of ice moving in the current, before freezing together in the fall.

**in wind:** Northeasterly wind on the shore, in from the ocean; on the Atlantic coast, a northeaster usually brings bad weather.

**Island, the:** Newfoundland.

**Islands, the:** Group of islands on the north shore of Lake Melville, about 12-15 miles from North West River.

**Klim:** Dried whole milk powder sold in large cans; "milk" spelled backwards.

**komatik:** Inuktitut word for sled pulled by dogs (or today, by snowmobile); usually 10-14 feet long.

***Kyle*:** A Reid Company coastal boat, sailing out of Carbonear, Newfoundland, that brought goods, mail, and passengers to and from Labrador from 1913 to the 1960s.

**landwash:** Shoreline; beach.

**leads:** A local term for valleys resulting from glacial action, generally running north and south and used to travel through the mountains and as a navigational guide; used here referring to the Mealy Mountains and caribou hunting.

**lop:** Rough water surface caused by short breaking waves

**Low, A.P. (1861-1942):** A late nineteenth-century and early twentieth-century explorer and, later, administrator with the Geological Survey of Canada who worked extensively on the Quebec-Labrador Peninsula. He mapped much of the Labrador interior and discovered large iron ore deposits in western Labrador, which eventually led to the development of mining operations there, and published his findings in his 1896 *Report on Explorations in the Labrador Peninsula*.

**MacMillan, Donald B. (1874-1970):** American explorer-adventurer and a pioneer in using radio and air flight in Arctic exploration who spent time in Labrador and Greenland in the 1920s; a member of Admiral Robert Peary's allegedly successful 1908-09 expedition to the North Pole, although MacMillan, because of frostbite, did not see the completion of the journey.

**maries:** Freshwater eels; morays.

**mild:** A brief period of fine warm weather that occurs during the cold-weather months.

**NALCO:** Newfoundland and Labrador Corporation, a provincial government development company established in 1951.

**nansearies:** Greater yellowlegs, a wading bird.

***naulak*:** The point or arrowhead of a spear used in seal hunting, with a line attached; this point detaches from the spear handle (*unak*) when it embeds in the target.

**oakum:** Loose fibre used for caulking and made from old rope that has been picked apart.

**on the last:** In later years.

**ouananiche:** A type of landlocked Atlantic salmon.

**outside:** Anywhere outside of Labrador.

**parbuckle:** A rope sling for raising heavy cylindrical objects (like a seal or a barrel) up an incline.

**partridge:** A game bird; willow ptarmigan is known locally as the white partridge; the spruce grouse is known locally as the spruce partridge.

**partridge hawk:** Gyrfalcon.

**paunch:** Eviscerate; usually refers to caribou or moose.

**pemmican:** Powdered dried caribou meat, made light for travel; may be mixed with bread crumbs or made into soup.

**piebirds:** Common goldeneye, a diving duck.

**portage:** Carrying canoes or cargo over land to avoid river obstacles like rapids, or between two bodies of water; the place where this carrying occurs.

**Privy Council:** Cabinet, i.e., the government, the body that advises the head of state of a nation; the British Privy Council was involved in settling the Quebec-Labrador boundary dispute.

**puddick:** Stomach of an animal, usually a seal; also called puttick or puttock.

**Rapids, the:** Narrow area of water between Grand Lake and Little Lake.

**redberries:** *Vaccinium vitis-idaea*; partridgeberries (Newfoundland), mountain cranberry or foxberry (N. America), lingonberry (Scandinavia); used for jam and desserts.

**rockweed**: Kelp, a seaweed; also known as Norwegian kelp or bladderwrack.

**scow:** Flat-bottomed boat with a blunt bow, towed by a motorboat and often used to haul bulk freight; used locally for bringing freight ashore from larger boats anchored in deep water, or for hauling firewood.

**serve:** Cover.

**sign:** Tracks or other marks to identify wildlife.

**slob:** Thick, slushy mixture of snow falling into cold water in the fall, before it turns into ice.

**Springs, the:** Natural springs on northeast shore of Little Lake.

**stake body truck:** A flat truck bed with sockets into which stakes may be fitted to support railings.

**steam:** Travel along in a boat.

**Strathcona:** Donald Alexander Smith, Lord Strathcona (1820-1914), fur trader, railroad financier, politician, and diplomat. The son of a Scottish tradesman, Smith joined the HBC in 1838 and worked his way from apprentice clerk to become Chief Commissioner in 1871; he was stationed at North West River from 1848 to 1869, where he established a farm and became Chief Factor of the Labrador District. Later, he became the only man to rise through the ranks, from grading muskrat pelts, to be appointed Governor of the Company. In the iconic 1885 photo of the "Last Spike" being driven for the transcontinental Canadian Pacific Railway, Smith is the man with sledgehammer driving the spike. Mentioned in Lydia Campbell's *Sketches of Labrador Life*.

**strike up:** Release the catch on a trap and close up the jaws so nothing can get in it; traps were left on site for use the next season.

**stuffing box:** Area around the driveshaft of the motor in older motorboats.

**swinged (singed) porcupine:** Traditional method of preparing porcupine; quills are singed and scraped off over a fire in preparation for cooking.

***taloouk*:** White screen used as a camouflage in seal hunting.

**Thevenet, Raoul (1875-1940):** Manager of Revillon Frères, the French fur-trading company established at North West River in 1901 for trading with Innu; Thevenet took charge in 1909; in later years, he and his family moved to North West River to work for the HBC and do some independent trading; their family spoke French and Innu.

**tide:** Current.

**tilt:** Small log cabin built and used by a trapper on his trapline, usually 7 or 8 feet square. Each trapline would have several tilts.

**tinker:** Northern razor-billed murre.

**trace:** Piece of line attached from each dog's harness to the bridle, which was attached to the komatik; in earlier days, these were always made of sealskin; later, bank line (cotton or hemp line) was used.

**tracking line:** Line tied to a canoe for hauling it through rapids; the line may have been tied to both ends of the canoe and controlled by one person on shore, or the line could be tied to the bow for hauling while one person in the canoe steered it.

**turr:** Atlantic common murre.

**ulus:** Inuit knives with crescent-shaped blades.

***unak*:** Spear, made of wood and an iron rod at the end, used in seal hunting, with a detachable point (*naulak*) attached to a 12-14-foot line.

**Watties:** Area on north shore of Grand Lake, about 25 miles from North West River.

**Young, Arminius:** Author of *A Methodist Missionary in Labrador* (1916); was in Labrador from 1903 to 1905.

# REFERENCES

Baikie, Margaret. *Labrador Memories: Reflections at Mulligan*. Happy Valley-Goose Bay: Them Days, n.d.

Blake, John. "Raymond Mesher," *Them Days* 16, 2 (1991): 28-29.

———. "Trappin' Grounds," *Them Days* 4, 3 (1979): 15-17.

Borlase, Tim, ed. *Songs of Labrador*. Fredericton, N.B.: Goose Lane Editions, 1993.

Bouchard, Serge. *Caribou Hunter: A Song of a Vanished Life*, trans. Joan Irving. Vancouver: Greystone Books, 2004.

Budgell, Leonard. *Arctic Twilight: Leonard Budgell and Canada's Changing North*. Toronto: Blue Butterfly Books, 2009.

Cabot, William Brooks. *In Northern Labrador*. London: J. Murray, 1912.

Campbell, Edna. "Aunt Edna Campbell," *Them Days* 17, 2 (1992): 29-33.

Campbell, Lydia. *Sketches of Labrador Life*. St. John's: Creative Publishers, 2000. First published 1894-95.

Cartwright, George. *Journal of Transactions and Events, during a Residence of Nearly Sixteen Years on the Coast of Labrador*, 3 vols. Newark, England, 1792.

Davies, K.G. *Northern Quebec and Labrador Journals and Correspondence: 1819-1835*. London: Hudson's Bay Record Society, 1963.

Goudie, Elizabeth, ed. *Woman of Labrador*. Introduction by David Zimmerly. Toronto: Peter Martin Associates, 1973.

Goudie, Harvey. "A Trapper's Life," *Them Days* 9, 1 (1983): 58-63.

Goudie, Horace. *Trails to Remember*. n.p.: Horace Goudie, 1991.

Grey, G.M. "Report on Trip to Labrador: May 19th-November 20th, 1929," *Them Days* 28, 1 (2003): 7-44.

Hamilton, Stephen. "How Did I Happen to Come to Labrador to Paint?" *Them Days* 27, 4 (2002): 37-45.

Henriksen, Georg. *I Dreamed the Animals: Kaniuetutat: The Life of an Innu Hunter*. London: Berghahn Books, 2008.

Holme, Randle F. *Some Things I Have Done*. London: Hepburn and Sons, 1949. A chapter in this book was first published in 1888: "A Journey in the Interior of Labrador," *Proceedings of the Royal Geographical Society*.

Hubbard, Mina Benson. *A Woman's Way through Unknown Labrador*. St. John's: Breakwater Books, 1983. Original edition published 1908.

"In the Matter of the Boundary between the Dominion of Canada and the Colony of Newfoundland on the Labrador Coast," *Them Days* 28, 4 (2004): 46-53.

Lethbridge, E. Chesley G.K. *A Life of Challenge (One Labradorian's Experience)*. n.p.: E. Chesley G.K. Lethbridge, 2007.

———. *Stories of the Past (Their Contribution to Society Will Not Be Forgotten)*. n.p.: E. Chesley G.K. Lethbridge, 2010.

Low, A.P. *Report on Explorations in the Labrador Peninsula along the East Main, Koksoak, Hamilton, Manicuagan and Portions of Other Rivers in 1892-93-94-95*. Geological Survey of Canada, vol. 8. Ottawa: S.E. Dawson, 1896.

Lyall, Ernie. *An Arctic Man*. Halifax: Formac Publishing, 1979.

Maggo, Paulus. *Remembering the Years of My Life: Journeys of a Labrador Inuit Hunter*, ed. Carol Brice-Bennett. St. John's: ISER Books, 1999.

McLean, Wallace. "Old Custom Trapping Laws," *Them Days* 2, 1 (1976): 5.

Merrick, Elliott. *True North*. New York: Charles Scribner's Sons, 1933.

———. *Northern Nurse*. New York: Charles Scribner's Sons, 1942.

Michelin, Stewart. "I Loved Furrin'," *Them Days* 2, 1 (1976): 7-10.

Montague, Austin. "Tha' Was Nothing," *Them Days* 1, 1 (1975): 10-13.

Montague, Austin, Jr., and Louie Montague. "Me an' Ockie an' Grampa," in Tim Borlase, ed., *Songs of Labrador*. Fredericton, N.B.: Goose Lane Editions, and the Labrador East Integrated School Board, 1993, p. 120.

Montague, John. "Trapping Was Our Life," *Them Days* 18, 4 (1993): 60-63.

Paddon, Harold G. *Green Woods and Blue Waters: Memories of Labrador*. St. John's: Breakwater Books, 1989.